Always delicious

favourite recipes from the *New Zealand Listener*

LAURAINE JACOBS

Photography by Liz Clarkson

Always delicious

favourite recipes from the *New Zealand Listener*

LAURAINE JACOBS

Photography by Liz Clarkson

First published in 2018 by Potton & Burton
98 Vickerman Street
PO Box 5128, Nelson, New Zealand
pottonandburton.co.nz

Text © Lauraine Jacobs
www.laurainejacobs.co.nz
Photography © Liz Clarkson
www.lizclarkson.co.nz

Design: Floor van Lierop

ISBN 978 0 947503 83 3

Printed in China by Midas Printing International Ltd

This book is copyright. Apart from any fair dealing for the purposes of private study, research, criticism or review, as permitted under the Copyright Act, no part may be reproduced by any process without the permission of the publisher.

CONTENTS

7 Introduction
8 Delicious, simple, fresh food

11 Sensational salads & vital vegetables
53 Things to savour
87 Something fishy
123 Meat matters
159 Winging it
189 Sweet as ...

224 Thanks
226 Inspiration, food heroes and suppliers
228 Index

INTRODUCTION

It's been an exciting and rewarding seven years for me, writing as a columnist in the *NZ Listener*. I regard my 1100 words every week for the 'Food' column as the dream job of New Zealand food writing. I enjoy working with chief editor Pamela Stirling and her talented team, who manage on a weekly basis to produce one of our country's most vital and intelligent current affairs, life and culture magazines.

For each Thursday morning deadline for my column, I have to plan, write and test the recipes, then style and photograph the dishes to illustrate my ramblings. There have been over 700 recipes delivered in those seven years. Occasionally I choose to share stunning recipes from cookbooks both local and international that I regard as books worth having, written by authors whose food I love. But 80 per cent of the fresh food you will see on the *Listener* pages comes from my own kitchen. For *Always Delicious*, I have chosen around 100 of these, the ones I consider some of my best. It was a tough task to narrow it down to this number, but I often say, most of us don't really need more than a basic repertoire of about 25 recipes that we're comfortable with and can reliably tweak according to the season.

I try to plan about two or three months ahead for the *Listener* columns, so I can spotlight seasonal ingredients, taking advantage of fruit and vegetables when they are not only at their best but also at their cheapest. There's no fun for cooks who, having decided on a recipe for dinner, find that the ingredients are out of season, have rocketed in price, or are even unobtainable. With each of these recipes I have signalled in which season they would be best cooked.

It's important to balance the sequence of the weeks so that no particular food dominates or, on the other hand, is overlooked. In this book, there's an equal emphasis on vegetables, fruit, meat, fish, dairy and grains, as there is in my columns. All of it gets seasonal treatment and suits my mantra of 'fresh and simple'.

I am also passionate about the New Zealand food scene, constantly championing our farmers, our artisan and larger food producers who all do a sterling job to bring the best food to our tables. Some of my columns involve gathering recipes and inspiration from our best chefs, too, as the restaurant and café scene in New Zealand is another of my passions. Over the past couple of decades, chefs have become more recognised for their innovation and dedication. They are the front line for presenting New Zealand food to locals and international visitors and they deserve our attention.

If you are a regular *NZ Listener* reader and have a favourite recipe that's not been included here, feel free to contact me, as lots of you do already. I trust you will enjoy this collection of recipes as much as I enjoy sharing them.

Lauraine Jacobs
Auckland, New Zealand, 2018
lauraine@laurainejacobs.co.nz

DELICIOUS, SIMPLE, FRESH FOOD

I'm often asked about my style of food and what I really enjoy. For someone as passionate about food as I am, this is easily explained. Food needs, first up, to be delicious. Secondly, whether I am cooking for myself, for family and friends or developing recipes for my readers, I want to keep things simple. If food is simple to prepare, it will be simple to eat, and everybody will love the cook who does that. And thirdly, it must be cooked with the best and freshest ingredients I can find.

This collection of my favourite recipes, ones I've loved so much I cook them constantly, is organised into six sections, with some cross-over of a few not easy to categorise. Salad and vegetables are at the core of every meal for me. As a Kiwi-raised girl who grew up with meat or protein at the centre of the dinner plate, I continue the habits of my lifetime, albeit with much smaller portions of lamb, beef, chicken or fish than when I started out cooking. There are always seasonal vegetables with my meals, and we eat vegetable-based dishes frequently.

I recognise baking is very much part of our New Zealand food culture, but baking or sweet things in my kitchen tends to only occur for special occasions. Nevertheless, the section of my dessert recipes is one to treasure. All food is good for you, unless you eat too much of it.

Of course, good food starts out with the best ingredients that can be purchased. In an ideal world, all produce we eat would be sourced close to home, straight from the garden or from a farmers' market. But it's not an ideal world and most cooks rely on shopping in their local supermarket for convenience, with food and household shopping all swept into one central weekly experience. I'm not a fan of prepared or processed food, with those stabilisers and preservatives needed to extend shelf life, nor do I eat take-out food. I firmly believe in cooking from scratch wherever possible and don't like to use flavour-added ingredients when I know I can add those flavours into my cooking myself.

But a good cook does more than just select fine ingredients. The senses play an important part too, and if the senses are engaged during cooking, the result will be even better. Smell, touch, listen and, most importantly, taste constantly as you go. It is impossible for any recipe creator to know exactly how the heat in your oven plays out, how thickly or finely you have cut your ingredients, and whether the seasoning suits your palate. Ultimately those things will affect the results, and with practice, the cooking process will become more enjoyable and your food will be brilliant. And never, never be afraid of adding salt.

There's a lot of focus on organically grown and sustainably using our land and resources in New Zealand. For those who can afford to be circumspect about the food choices they make, these issues are important. In the past we neglected the environment to our shame, but I believe we're getting back on track and making changes that will see our land productive for generations to come (as long as we don't give our best-growing soils over to housing developments).

The cook who cares needs to know the stories behind their food purchases. Restaurants with smart chefs have been doing this for some time, and it's common to be told about the provenance of the items on any menu. Our large food companies take care to offer food that's safe but they can have blind spots about what's good for our bodies and our health. Shop carefully, don't buy more than you can eat, don't accept inferior or stale produce, and get interested in the stories of the producers and farmers when you buy your food.

Seasonal, local eating is at the heart of my thinking – but as a food-exporting country we must be respectful of the balance of trade and also eat imported food. I buy internationally sourced ingredients like rice, coffee, flour, sugar, tropical fruits, occasional wild-caught prawns, exotic vinegars, chocolate and more. I love to travel about the country and overseas, finding inspiration in eating out, understanding the regional fare that reflects the local terroir and immersing myself in others' food cultures. Many of my recipes reflect these travels.

Most importantly, I hope some of these recipes will have you energised to get into the kitchen, be excited about cooking and really enjoy delicious food. But please think of these recipes as guides – not dogma. Ingredients in most savoury cooking can be substituted when there's something that's not available, is out of season or maybe something that you dislike. Feel free to experiment, for it's my view that a good cook is someone who reads a recipe, is inspired to cook and then pushes on to develop his or her own version of it. Do remember, however, that baking is akin to chemistry and the carefully tested equations of a baking recipe cannot be meddled with.

I have always thought as a food writer that recipes are gifts. Gifts from my kitchen to yours. Please enjoy this book filled with my gifts.

SECTION 1
Sensational salads & vital vegetables

- 12   Spring green salad
- 14   Avocado & caramelised pineapple salad
- 16   *Food Talk: Salad days*
- 18   Roasted fennel & prawn salad
- 20   Sardine & egg salad
- 22   Ham, mozzarella & tomato salad
- 24   Grilled vegetable & black rice salad
- 26   Aubergine & pepper stew with chickpeas & basil
- 28   Roasted aubergine with red onions, yogurt & lemon
- 30   Carrot, cheese & coriander fritters
- 32   Roast squash wedges with pine nuts, yogurt & sumac
- 34   Baked kale with potatoes, olives & garlic
- 36   Persimmon & salami salad with balsamic dressing
- 38   Kohlrabi & apple salad
- 40   Rice & quinoa salad with beetroot & carrots
- 42   Roast leek, mandarin & egg salad
- 44   Orange, fennel & pomegranate salad
- 46   Buttery braised fennel
- 48   Warm cauliflower salad
- 50   Roasted golden cauliflower

Spring heralds new growth and one of the most prized seasonal vegetables: asparagus. I cannot resist the first of the harvest when it arrives in my local store, and confess to paying pretty outrageous prices for just six or seven spears so I can get a taste of this treat that I hanker for. But a few weeks on, asparagus will come crashing down in price, to make an almost nightly appearance on my dinner menus. If I am serving a salad as part of a main course, I will often just stick to leafy plants with a handful of fresh herbs straight from my garden to boost the flavour. But as a simple lunch or an interesting, light entrée, I like to add a few blanched vegetables, and asparagus in season is a must-have. Herbs that have burst into flower, such as borage, chives or nasturtiums, will add striking colour and extra taste.

Spring green salad

SERVES 6
WINE SUGGESTION: RIESLING
BEST IN SPRING

10 asparagus spears, neatly cut into 5cm lengths

a handful of snow peas

2 cups assorted lettuce leaves

1 cup watercress, thicker stalks removed

1 cup broad beans, shelled, blanched and hulled

2 oranges

3 spring onions

borage flowers for garnish

dressing:

1 orange, juice and finely grated rind

juice of 1 lemon

12 saffron threads

salt and pepper

1 tsp mustard

4 tbsp extra virgin olive oil

pinch of sugar to taste

To blanch the asparagus and snow peas, bring a large pot of well-salted water to boil. Once at a rolling boil, toss the asparagus and snow peas in and allow to simmer for 1–2 minutes, then remove, drain and immediately plunge into icy cold water. They will retain crispness and bright green colour.

Wash the lettuce leaves and watercress and dry in a salad spinner or shake between two clean tea towels.

Toss the leaves into a wide, shallow serving bowl and add the broad beans, asparagus and snow peas. You can make the salad ahead to this point and cover with plastic wrap and refrigerate for a few hours.

Peel the oranges with a knife, removing all the white pith, and cut into neat segments. Chop the spring onions into pieces.

Make the dressing by mixing the orange and lemon juice with the grated orange rind, saffron threads, salt, pepper, mustard, olive oil and sugar together. Taste and adjust with extra salt or sugar if needed.

Just before serving toss the leaves and vegetables together with the dressing. To finish, scatter over the spring onions and orange segments and decorate with a few borage flowers or other herb flowers.

Pineapple is one of those fruits we take for granted, not unlike bananas. It's rare to find pineapple (or bananas) growing anywhere in New Zealand apart from the Far North and they're certainly not a large commercial crop. Having been brought up on pineapples as a child, when our grandmother regularly would send cases of them to us from her home in Tonga, I love them. I was sorry to see our border authority ban importing them unless their spiky tops had been cut off, but guarding our vital horticulture industries is paramount. And the taste of the pineapple is not affected. This gorgeous salad will be a surprise to many with the fresh, caramelised pineapple. It makes a great entrée or main course when served with some crusty bread and fresh butter.

Avocado & caramelised pineapple salad

SERVES 6
WINE SUGGESTION: GEWÜRZTRAMINER
BEST IN SPRING / EARLY SUMMER

½ fresh pineapple, peeled

2 tbsp brown sugar

2 tbsp butter

3 firm but ripe avocados

100g creamy blue cheese

½ red onion

1 small red chilli

2 cups fresh red salad leaves, washed

Dressing:

1 orange, zest and juice

1 tsp ground cumin

1 small chilli, finely chopped

4 tbsp avocado oil

salt and freshly ground black pepper

Remove the core from the pineapple and cut the flesh into 3cm cubes and sprinkle with brown sugar. Put a frying pan onto heat and add the butter. When the butter is melted and starting to sizzle, toss the pineapple in and fry over gentle heat until they are caramelised on all sides. Allow to cool.

Peel the avocados and cut into 2–3cm cubes. Break the cheese into small pieces and slice the onion paper-thin. Slice the chilli into thin pieces.

Make the dressing by shaking all the dressing ingredients together in a jar.

To serve, line a flat serving plate with the fresh salad leaves. Toss the avocado, pineapple, blue cheese, chilli and red onion on top of the leaves. Drizzle over the dressing and serve at once.

Food Talk // Salad days

It's usually the arrival of warmer weather that brings thoughts of salad. But whatever the season, a salad will always be welcome, served alongside comforting, sustaining food in the winter months, or as a light, crisp bowl of leaves freshly plucked from a spring garden.

The French have a wonderful term, salade composée, which holds its place at the dining table, put together with the freshest of leaves as a base and then various vegetables and meats atop, dressed with a delicious salad dressing. These salads are a luncheon or light-dinner dish, with slices of crusty baguette to mop up the delicious vinaigrette.

As spring advances, it's worth incorporating the harvest of asparagus, broad beans, baby beans and the first of the root crops – baby potatoes, spring carrots and tender green leaves.

The salad must be balanced, however. Vegetables may be raw, blanched or even roasted but they should be chosen to emphasise salty, sweet, bitter and acidic notes. This can be aided by a dressing that provides these flavours. The texture should be considered, and don't forget about colour. A salad should look inviting, and provide a chance for the cook to think like an artist.

Fresh salads can provide the answer to easy summer meals when heat and humidity sap our energy. Our bodies cry out for something light and delicious.

To build my salad I always start by covering the platter with fresh leaves. Next, I add a vegetable in season – this may be chunks of avocado, ripe tomatoes, fresh corn, radishes, sugar snap or fresh peas, blanched beans, roasted peppers or fried courgettes. Later in the season or early winter, I will add florets of broccoli or cauliflower or roasted potato, pumpkin and kumara. Other vegetables can be beetroot, and carrots either grated raw or steamed, and kale.

For texture, add toasted or raw nuts, croutons of baked or lightly fried sourdough bread, seeds of all description (pomegranates are wondrous this year), or sprouts.

Herbs picked from the garden are essential for a fresh salad. Keep to the soft-leafed herbs because thyme, rosemary and sage are too tough to eat raw. Choose mint, basil, chervil, parsley, coriander, dill or tarragon to add freshness and zing to the combination of leaves and vegetables. Microgreens or herb flowers can add interest and colour.

A salad can become a hearty meal by adding a little meat, carbohydrates or protein, and if you want, cooked pasta, beans, grains or couscous make a substantial salad.

Perhaps the most important part of the salad is the dressing. It should never dominate nor be too heavy, acidic or too sweet. If all the ingredients are robust, toss the dressing through well ahead of serving time so everything gets a chance to absorb the flavours. But if using soft leaves or ingredients already rather moist, toss the dressing through immediately before you serve it.

Flavours of Asia dressing

1 lime

small bunch of fresh coriander

4 tbsp soy sauce

4 tbsp fish sauce

3 tbsp sesame oil

100ml grapeseed oil

small pinch of brown sugar

Finely grate zest of a lime and squeeze all the juice into a screw-top jar. Chop the coriander finely and add with the zest and remaining ingredients, and shake well. Use this dressing judiciously and store in the refrigerator for 2–3 weeks. This dressing can be used for green salads, especially with cucumber, and salads that have lightly blanched beans, peas, courgettes, broccoli, mushrooms, spinach leaves, carrots and Asian greens.

Makes about 1 cup

Classic French vinaigrette

2 tbsp white wine vinegar

1 tsp Dijon-style mustard

pinch sugar

6 tbsp extra virgin olive oil

1 tsp salt

freshly ground black pepper

Place the vinegar, mustard and the sugar in a bowl or small jar and mix well so the mustard and sugar completely dissolve. Add the oil, salt and a generous grind of black pepper, and whisk or shake the ingredients together until thoroughly combined. Store in the refrigerator in a screw-top jar. Use this dressing on any classic salad, especially leafy green leaves that have been washed and dried well. Only dress the salad immediately before serving.

Makes about half a cup

Orange & honey vinaigrette

1 orange

1 tbsp runny honey

1 tsp finely grated ginger

6 tbsp (100ml) avocado oil

1 tsp salt

freshly ground black pepper

2 tbsp fresh mint leaves, finely chopped

Finely grate the zest and squeeze the juice of the orange. Place this in a screw-top jar with all the other ingredients. Shake well. Store for 1–2 weeks. This dressing goes particularly well with any salad that has fruit in it, as the lack of vinegar and the sweetness of the orange and honey really complement chunks of papaya, mango, pineapple, apple, pears, figs and peaches. It is superb with tomato and avocado salads.

Makes half a cup

Prawns are an enigmatic food for me as, despite the wealth of fish and shellfish we can choose from, the New Zealand coast is not home to a bountiful supply of fresh prawns or shrimps. Almost every prawn, apart from a minimal number grown in the thermal area around Taupō, is imported. I always look for Australian wild-caught prawns that have been imported frozen. They are generally superior in taste and texture to Asian-farmed prawns. This salad is one of my favourites, made with roasted rather than raw fennel. The roasting process makes the fennel much more flavourful and sweet.

Roasted fennel & prawn salad

SERVES 4
WINE SUGGESTION: ZINGY RIESLING
BEST IN SPRING

2 small fennel bulbs

4 tbsp grapeseed oil

salt and freshly ground black pepper

200g raw prawns or shrimp, shelled

2 handfuls mesclun or rocket leaves

1 large carrot, peeled

1 cup broad beans, shelled

1 cup Italian parsley leaves, stalks removed

Dressing:

1 orange

1 tsp Dijon mustard

2 tbsp finely chopped parsley

5 tbsp extra virgin olive oil

salt and freshly ground black pepper

Preheat the oven to 180°C.

Wash the fennel bulbs well and slice thickly. Place them in an ovenproof dish with the oil and roast for 20 minutes until soft (alternatively you could do this in a frying pan over low heat on the stove top). For the last five minutes of the cooking time, toss in the shrimp or prawns and cook until they become opaque.

Wash the mesclun or rocket and dry thoroughly. Using a potato peeler, cut long ribbons of carrot. Remove the broad beans from their pods and steam for about 3 minutes.

Remove strips of orange zest from the orange with a fine zester and blanch these in boiling water for 30 seconds.

Make the dressing by shaking all the ingredients together in a screw-top jar.

To assemble the salad, pile the leaves on to a deep serving platter or bowl. Toss in the fennel, prawns, carrot strips, broad beans and parsley leaves.

Add the orange zest strips to the dressing and toss gently to coat all ingredients.

Serve at once as a lunch or light dinner, accompanied by slices of fresh wholemeal bread.

I like to keep a few tins and jars of tinned salmon, sardines, octopus, anchovies and bottled tuna, chickpeas, olives, capers and butter beans in my pantry for those unexpected occasions. Consider buying these items when you're a bit flush as it is worth keeping the highest quality of these special foods. This is one of those cupboard go-to recipes where a few salad ingredients are brightened up to make a full meal with eggs and sardines.

Sardine & egg salad

SERVES 2
WINE SUGGESTION: PINOT GRIS
BEST IN EVERY SEASON

3 eggs

1 head soft, leafy green lettuce

1 avocado

2 plump radishes

1 tin sardines in oil

1 tbsp finely chopped preserved lemon

½ cup Italian parsley leaves, roughly chopped

salt and pepper

balsamic glaze

Simmer the eggs in water for 7–8 minutes, then plunge into cold water to stop them cooking further.

While the eggs are boiling you can prepare the rest of the salad. Break the lettuce into leaves and wash well, drying with a tea towel or in a salad spinner.

Peel the avocado and slice into chunks.

Cut the radish into paper-thin slices.

Peel the eggs and cut each egg in half.

Lay the salad leaves on a platter and arrange the avocado, radishes, sardines and eggs on top.

Sprinkle with the preserved lemon, parsley and salt and pepper to taste. Spoon over some of the sardine oil from the can and add a drizzle of balsamic glaze.

I love the variety of salad leaves we can choose from and I grow several varieties in my garden, choosing plants with leaves that can be cut and will regenerate rather than those that heart up and need to be cut at the base. This red, soft-leafed lettuce does really well, and just a few plants in the garden will keep us going for weeks. Mozzarella cheese has become very popular, and it's worth seeking out the freshest balls of this light, squeaky cheese. The best is made from buffalo milk and there are several buffalo farms now supplying milk to cheesemakers. There are also excellent cow mozzarella cheeses locally and imported from Italy. Fresh mozzarella is packed in tubs with plenty of brine to keep it fresh. Do not think you can substitute the harder yellow cheese labelled mozzarella. This should be reserved for cooking on pizzas and other baked dishes.

Ham, mozzarella & tomato salad

SERVES 2 BUT CAN BE SCALED UP
WINE SUGGESTION: CHILLED ROSÉ
BEST IN SUMMER AND AUTUMN

2 cups red leafy lettuce

1 cup peas, fresh or frozen

1 cup baby or cherry tomatoes

6 slices ham, thinly sliced

1 ball mozzarella cheese

½ cup fresh mint leaves, some sliced finely

Dressing:

1 tbsp red wine vinegar

3 tbsp extra virgin olive oil

1 tsp Dijon mustard

pinch of sugar

salt and pepper

Separate the lettuce leaves, wash well and dry with a tea towel or in a salad spinner.

Briefly blanch the peas in boiling water and cool immediately in cold water.

Wash the tomatoes and cut each into two.

Lay the lettuce leaves on a salad platter or shallow bowl. Roll the ham slices up and nestle them into the lettuce with the tomatoes.

Break the mozzarella into pieces with your hands and add these pieces to the salad. Scatter over the peas and the mint.

Mix the vinegar, oil, mustard, sugar, and salt and pepper together so they are well combined and pour over the salad.

This is a wonderful recipe. It will make a substantial salad that's easy to prepare ahead or to transport when you're asked to contribute to a meal where a crowd is expected. Black rice has a delicious nutty flavour and is too often overlooked.

Grilled vegetable & black rice salad

SERVES 6–8
WINE SUGGESTION: A HEARTY RED WINE SUCH AS CABERNET MERLOT
BEST IN SUMMER/EARLY AUTUMN

1 cup black rice

2 cups water

2 ears corn, shucked

2 sweet red peppers, seeds removed

6 small beetroot, peeled

3 carrots, peeled

3 courgettes

4 tbsp extra virgin olive oil

salt and freshly ground black pepper

1 cup rocket leaves

To finish:

2 tbsp balsamic vinegar

3 tbsp extra virgin olive oil

1 lemon, grated zest and juice

salt and freshly ground black pepper

Preheat the oven to 180°C.

Wash the rice well under running water in a sieve. Tip into a heavy-based saucepan and cover with the water. Bring the rice to a simmer, reduce the heat, clamp the lid of the saucepan on and allow the rice to cook for about 30 minutes until all the water is absorbed, the rice is soft and the grains are separated. Stir well with a fork so the grains do not stick together and keep aside to cool.

Meanwhile cut the corn into 3cm pieces, slice the peppers, and cut or slice the beetroot, carrots and courgettes into even chunks. Place them all together in a roasting pan and toss in the olive oil with a sprinkling of salt and pepper. Roast for about 30–35 minutes or until the vegetables are soft when pierced with a fork. Remove from the oven and cool.

Wash and dry the rocket leaves and trim off any long stalks.

Prepare the dressing by mixing the balsamic, olive oil, lemon zest and juice with salt and pepper to taste in a small screw-top jar.

Pile the rice on a dish. Add most of the vegetables and rocket. Add the dressing and toss everything together. Finally garnish the top with the remaining vegetables and rocket.

Many cooks salt their aubergines in the belief that salt draws out bitterness. In summer, salting sun-ripened, outdoor-grown aubergines before cooking is unnecessary. However, salt does draw the moisture out to make the flesh firmer and not absorb quite so much oil in the cooking process. The essential thing is to cook the aubergine thoroughly before adding to any dish. The spongy flesh needs to become silken and melting. A few years back, on an olive oil estate in Sicily, I was invited to help with dinner and was given a pile of small aubergines to be halved, pierced with cloves of garlic and cooked in a pan of hot olive oil. A salutary lesson in adding flavour by careful cooking, for those aubergines softened up in the oil before being added to a pot of gently simmering fresh tomatoes and basil. The combination was heavenly. Since then I have fried my aubergines in an extravagant amount of oil before using them in any dish. You can also slow-roast aubergines, but whether roasted in the oven for 45 minutes or turned over the flame of a charcoal-fuelled grill (a better bet), the flesh will become sensuous and fragrant. This recipe can be prepared ahead as this allows the flavours to meld together.

Aubergine & pepper stew with chickpeas & basil

SERVES 4
WINE SUGGESTION: CHARDONNAY
BEST IN LATE SUMMER/AUTUMN

4–5 tbsp extra virgin olive oil

2 medium aubergines, cut into 6cm chunks

2 red capsicums, finely sliced

1 large onion, finely sliced

6 garlic cloves, peeled

500g ripe tomatoes, chopped

1 teaspoon salt

small pinch sugar

10cm strip lemon rind

1 bay leaf

1 cup dry white wine

a handful of fresh basil leaves

450g can chickpeas, drained

Heat the oil in a heavy frying pan until medium hot. Add the aubergine chunks and sauté until golden, turning frequently. Remove the aubergines to drain on paper towels.

Add more olive oil to the pan if necessary and add the sliced peppers, onions and whole garlic cloves. Cook gently over low heat for 10–15 minutes or until the mixture softens. Add the tomatoes, salt, sugar, lemon rind, bay leaf and wine. Bring to a slow simmer and return the aubergines to the mixture with the basil. Simmer together for 15 minutes until soft and aromatic. Add the drained chickpeas and continue to simmer the stew for a further 5 minutes. To serve, turn into a shallow, heated serving dish.

One of the most influential cooks on the current food scene is the talented Yotam Ottolenghi. Anyone who has visited his food stores in London or knows his recipes will understand why. Tempting, colourful, flavourful food is piled high, the baking is exquisite, and his salads are a carefully thought-out jumble of Middle Eastern/Israeli-inspired flavours and textures, all made with fresh ingredients. He has brought fragrant spices into cooking like no other contemporary chef. This aubergine recipe is Ottolenghi-inspired and represents everything I love about his books and his food.

Roasted aubergine with red onions, yogurt & lemon

SERVES 4
WINE SUGGESTION: DRY GEWÜRZTRAMINER
BEST IN AUTUMN

4 small aubergines

150ml olive oil

salt and freshly ground black pepper

3 red onions, finely sliced

1 tsp ground cumin

1 tsp sumac

4 tbsp Greek-style unsweetened yogurt

1 medium lemon

¼ preserved lemon, finely sliced

parsley for garnish

Preheat the oven to 190°C.

Slice each aubergine in half, score the surface in a crisscross pattern and brush each with a little of the oil, seasoning with salt and pepper. Place in a roasting dish and bake for 35–40 minutes until golden brown and soft. This could be done over a charcoal grill for even more flavour.

Meanwhile, heat the remaining oil in a heavy frying pan until medium hot. Add the sliced onions, turn the heat down and cook for 10 minutes until really soft and beginning to brown. Add the cumin and sumac and cook a further 2 minutes. Remove from the heat.

Make a yogurt and lemon sauce by placing the yogurt in a bowl. Grate the zest of the lemon and add to the yogurt with the lemon juice. Taste, add salt if necessary and a good pinch of freshly ground black pepper.

Transfer the aubergine halves from the oven onto a serving dish. Spoon over the lemon and yogurt sauce. Pile the onions on top with a little preserved lemon, and parsley leaves.

Serve as a starter or as an accompaniment to roast lamb.

The carrot is an unsung hero in the vegetable world. Available year-round, it is inexpensive, nutritious, tasty when eaten raw, provides a note of sweetness when cooked, and more recently is the perfect ingredient in freshly pressed juice. Carrots were not always orange. Food historians agree that the first carrots, with branched purple roots, originated in Afghanistan, before they spread eastwards to India, China and Japan in the twelfth century and west to continental Europe in the fourteenth century. In the seventeenth century Dutch horticulturalists hybridised the popular bright orange colour that has become the accepted form of this vegetable. Recently, as the foodie world clamours for authenticity and exclusivity, many new cultivars have emerged: violet, purple, white, red, yellow and orange colours, and both baby and slender shapes.

Carrot, cheese & coriander fritters

MAKES 10 OR 12 FRITTERS
WINE SUGGESTION: RIESLING
BEST IN EVERY SEASON

500g peeled carrots

2 eggs

3 tbsp flour

salt and freshly ground pepper

4 spring onions, finely chopped

½ cup coriander leaves

150g creamy feta cheese

2 limes

coconut or grapeseed oil for frying

Grate the carrots into long thin shreds (best achieved by using the fine grating blade of a food processor). Put the carrots aside while you make the fritter batter.

In a medium bowl, beat the eggs with the flour, salt and pepper until well mixed and free of lumps.

Add the grated carrot, chopped spring onions and coriander leaves to the batter, turning it with your fingertips so it mixes well. Chop the feta into tiny cubes about 1cm, and add with the zest and juice of one of the limes to the carrot batter.

Heat a large frying pan and add about 3 tablespoons of oil to medium heat. Take enough carrot batter to fit in the palm of your hand, pressing it together to form a fritter-like shape. Drop the balls into the hot oil in the pan, cooking 3 or 4 at a time, pushing them down with a metal spatula or fish slice to flatten. Cook for 3 minutes on the first side then flip each over and cook until the fritters are golden and cooked through. Remove and place on a paper towel and keep warm.

Repeat this process until all the batter is used. You may have to wipe the pan out after the second batch and use more oil as it can get rather greasy.

To serve, place on plates with wedges of the remaining lime.

This is a simple but tasty way to serve pumpkin or squash. It is the perfect accompaniment to lamb, whether you're roasting a leg or serving some cutlets or chops. The roasting process definitely brings out the sweetness in the squash or pumpkin. There are plenty of varieties of squash that ripen in the autumn, but my favourite is the lovely grey-skinned pumpkin, which also makes a fine soup. I never remove the skin when I am roasting this delicious vegetable. I just give it a good scrub and find if it is cooked to a crisp, the skin is good to eat, too.

Roast squash wedges with pine nuts, yogurt & sumac

SERVES 6–8
WINE SUGGESTION: SYRAH
BEST IN AUTUMN/WINTER

1 medium squash or half a small pumpkin

3 tbsp olive oil

salt and freshly ground black pepper

3 tbsp fresh thyme, finely chopped

4 tbsp Greek-style unsweetened yogurt

4 tbsp pine nuts, lightly toasted

1 tsp sumac

Preheat the oven to 200°C.

Cut the squash or pumpkin into large wedges, and remove the seeds and stringy centre. Sprinkle each wedge with olive oil, salt, plenty of black pepper and chopped thyme.

Place in a roasting dish and roast for 30–40 minutes, depending on the thickness, until the flesh is tender and the skin is brittle.

To serve, place on a large platter, drizzle the yogurt over the centre of each wedge and top with pine nuts and a sprinkling of sumac.

I admit that kale is not amongst my top ten – or even top twenty – vegetables. It's a tough customer, chewy and bitter when raw, and it takes an awful amount of cooking time to render it tender. Personally, I believe it should never be served raw unless it is a selection of the tiniest new leaves that have been freshly plucked from the garden. However, this recipe with kale is a winner. Credit must go to Elizabeth Schneider, as it is based on a recipe in her wonderful book *Vegetables from Amaranth to Zucchini: The Essential Reference*. This almost encyclopediac volume is a constant source of reference for me. Try cooking this dish, and I am sure, like me, you will see kale in a new light.

Baked kale with potatoes, olives & garlic

SERVES 4
WINE SUGGESTION: PINOT NOIR
BEST IN WINTER

750g kale or cavolo nero

750g small red potatoes

2 tbsp extra virgin olive oil, plus extra for drizzling

20 pitted black olives

2 garlic cloves, chopped

½ cup water

¼ cup vermouth

freshly ground black pepper

lemon wedges

Preheat the oven to 160°C.

Wash the kale well in plenty of water and drain. Strip out the thickest stems, but there's no need to remove the smaller stalks. Slice the kale into 2cm slices.

Scrub the potatoes and cut into thin slices.

Heat the oil in a large casserole dish. Add the garlic and stir until it softens. Add the potatoes, tossing well. Add the kale, olives, water and vermouth and bring to a simmer.

Cover the dish tightly and bake in the oven until the potatoes are just tender (about 35–40 minutes), shaking occasionally.

Add a little extra olive oil to finish and serve hot or at room temperature with freshly ground black pepper and lemon wedges.

There are two distinct types of persimmon – the first is the traditional oval-pointed fruit, mostly the Hachiya variety, which should be eaten when ripe, with an almost jelly-like consistency. Before it is fully ripened with a soft interior, it has a nasty tannic astringency. Often this type of persimmon is found in old gardens and orchards, with brilliantly coloured autumn leaves that make a great ornamental show. It is so misunderstood it is rarely found commercially. It is one of those foods that is either loved or despised with no middle ground. Fortunately, the non-astringent persimmon, fuyu, is a delight to eat. It has a crisp texture, with the crunchiness making it ideal for use in salads or as a snack, just like a fresh apple. It can be eaten as soon as it is picked when the skin is turning from light orange to a dark saffron-red. When choosing the fuyu persimmon, make sure the skin is shiny, the fruit is heavy and the calyx on the top is bright green, not brown. Store in a single layer at room temperature and eat while still firm. Like the astringent variety these fruit will become jelly-like if left too long. The persimmon's flavour is quite subtle, with a lovely perfume. Horizontal slices have a lovely star effect in the middle. Here the persimmon pairs beautifully with prosciutto or ham as a delicate starter.

Persimmon & salami salad with balsamic dressing

SERVES 4
WINE SUGGESTION: RIESLING
BEST IN AUTUMN/EARLY WINTER

2 cups wild rocket leaves

2 baby gem lettuces

2 persimmons, peeled and cut into wedges

20 thin slices mild salami

150g creamy blue cheese

Dressing:

2 tbsp balsamic vinegar

4 tbsp olive oil

½ tsp salt

freshly ground black pepper

Wash the rocket and lettuce leaves well and dry in a tea towel or salad spinner.

Arrange the leaves on a serving platter and scatter over the persimmon wedges. Nestle the salami into the leaves amongst the persimmon.

Break the cheese into neat little nuggets and tuck these into the salad.

Make the dressing by shaking the balsamic, oil, salt and pepper together in a screw-top jar.

Finish the salad by spooning the dressing over everything and serve at once as a starter or with some crusty bread as a lunch main course.

Kohlrabi is another uncommonly eaten vegetable that's versatile and in season in winter months. A member of the brassica family, the leaves are edible, but the main attraction of this sputnik-like vegetable is the bulb, which, in reality, is the stem of the plant. It grows in most climates around New Zealand and when I enquired at my local vegetable store in autumn, the owner had no trouble sourcing both pale green and violet-coloured varieties. It is at its best when peeled and cut into thin slices to be served raw in salads or as a snack with a creamy blue or goat-cheese dip. It can also be grated for tossing into slaws or salads. Add kohlrabi to stir-fry vegetables, soups and braises. The pieces will require about 10–15 minutes and should remain slightly crisp. The flavour is not strong so a little aromatic spice such as nutmeg, ginger or cumin will boost the taste, and woody herbs like rosemary, sage or thyme pair nicely with kohlrabi.

Kohlrabi & apple salad

SERVES 4
WINE SUGGESTION: PINOT GRIS
BEST IN AUTUMN

1 cup fresh walnuts

2 bulbs of kohlrabi

2 apples

½ cup parsley leaves

Vinaigrette:

1 lemon, juice and grated zest

3 tbsp walnut oil

salt and freshly ground black pepper

Heat the oven to 170°C.

Place the walnuts in a roasting pan and bake for 5–7 minutes or until the walnuts just start to colour. Remove at once.

Peel the kohlrabi and slice as thinly as possible using a sharp knife or a mandolin.

Cut the apples into quarters, remove the cores and cut into 1cm matchstick pieces.

Chop the parsley roughly.

To make the vinaigrette, mix the lemon juice, walnut oil, salt and pepper together until well combined.

To assemble the salad, lay the sliced kohlrabi on a flat salad plate, scatter over a layer of apple. Top with walnuts and parsley and finally drizzle the vinaigrette over everything.

Serve to accompany grilled steak or roast pork.

This recipe was created with freshness in mind and will be perfect as a light meal or to accompany a simple outdoor barbecue. The inspiration came from Annie Guinness, my friend and a superb cook, who brought a similar salad to a birthday party we held for my daughter. In spring and summer, many herbs and vegetables produce flowers in abundance, and it's interesting just how tasty herb flowers can be, with most having a more intense aroma and taste than the herb leaves.

Rice & quinoa salad with beetroot & carrots

SERVES 10
WINE SUGGESTION: PINOT BLANC
BEST IN AUTUMN/WINTER

1 cup brown rice and quinoa mix (or just use quinoa)

2 cups water

salt to taste

2 sweet red peppers

1 cup freshly chopped herbs (parsley, mint, basil and chives)

2 small Lebanese cucumbers, diced

2 tbsp wine vinegar

6 tbsp extra virgin olive oil

salt and freshly ground black pepper

3 large carrots

2 tbsp grapeseed or light vegetable oil

1 tbsp freshly grated turmeric (or dried)

pinch of cumin seeds

2 large beetroot

4 tbsp pine nuts, lightly roasted

3 spring onions, chopped

wild flowers and leaves for garnish (nasturtiums, herb flowers)

Place the rice and quinoa mix in a sieve and rinse under running cold water. Drain and transfer to a medium saucepan, add the water and a little salt. Place the pan over a high heat. Once the rice is at a rolling boil, turn the heat low and cover. Let the rice and quinoa simmer until all the water is absorbed (about 18–20 minutes). Remove from the heat and set the rice aside.

Roast the peppers in 160°C oven until the skins blister and darken, about 15–20 minutes. Remove, cool and strip the seeds from the interior. Cut the peppers into strips.

Place the rice and quinoa in a bowl and add the pepper, herbs and cucumber. Toss in the vinegar, oil, season to taste, and mix everything well together. Refrigerate this if you plan to serve the salad later in the day.

Cut the carrots into matchsticks. Heat the grapeseed oil, add turmeric and cook until it starts to release its aroma, then add carrot with cumin and a pinch of salt. Cook gently until the carrot starts to soften. Remove from the heat and cool.

Peel the beetroot and grate quite finely or cut into thin matchsticks.

Pile the rice mixture into the centre of a serving platter. Surround with a ring of carrot and then add the beetroot around the outside. Strew pine nuts and spring onions over the top and decorate with nasturtiums.

Leeks, the most versatile and mild member of the allium group, deserve pride of place amongst the array of winter vegetables. They have a sweetness and distinction that far outweighs the onion, and with gentle cooking develop a silky, mellow flavour that adds a pleasing dimension to soups and casseroles. Although available year-round, the leek's peak season is the winter months. In early spring, smaller, sweeter leeks appear and their pale tenderness is great for recipes where the leek is to be cooked whole. Leeks push themselves up through the dirt as they grow, so it is inevitable that dirt and mud is trapped between the layers. The best way to deal with this is to slit the leek along its length to within 5cm of the base and fan the layers out underneath plenty of cold running water. Soak the washed leek for a further ten minutes so any remaining particles float away. When using whole leeks, trim the roots away without completely cutting off the base so that the leek holds together.

Roast leek, mandarin & egg salad

SERVES 4
WINE SUGGESTION: RIESLING
BEST IN WINTER

8 smallish leeks

2 tbsp olive oil

salt and pepper

2 eggs

4 small mandarins

3 tbsp pitted olives, chopped

½ cup mint leaves, stalks removed

Dressing:

1 small mandarin

3 tbsp extra virgin olive oil

1 lemon, zest and juice

salt and pepper

Pre-heat the oven to 180°C.

Scrub and trim the leeks neatly, leaving whole. Toss the leeks in oil in a roasting pan and sprinkle with pepper and salt. Roast for 15–20 minutes until tender and sweet.

Meanwhile, hard boil the eggs (9 minutes), and then plunge immediately into cold water to prevent the eggs forming a dark ring between the yolk and white. Peel four of the mandarins, taking care to remove all the pith. Cut through the middle horizontally and cut again in half. Chop the hard-boiled eggs and olives roughly.

To make the dressing, lightly zest the lemon and mandarin, then squeeze the juice of both into a bowl, add salt and pepper and whisk in the olive oil. Taste and adjust the seasoning if necessary.

To serve, place two warm leeks on each plate, arrange the mandarin halves, olives and chopped egg casually over the top. Spoon the dressing over and add mint leaves to garnish.

This salad is simple to prepare and is one of my favourites when I want something light to go with meat, chicken or fish. It looks really pretty when decorated with the pomegranate seeds (arils). Try to cut the fennel as thinly as possible. I have a handy Japanese mandolin that will cut paper-thin slices, but failing that, make sure your knives are razor sharp. A sharp knife is one of the most essential pieces of kitchen equipment and it is certainly worth sharpening your knives at least once a month.

Orange, fennel & pomegranate salad

SERVES 4–6
WINE SUGGESTION: RIESLING
BEST IN WINTER

4 juicy navel oranges

2 small bulbs fennel

3 tbsp fresh pomegranate arils (seeds)

1 tbsp mint, chopped or whole if small

Dressing:

1 lemon, juice only

1 tbsp aromatic honey

1 tsp orange flower water (or zest of one extra orange)

2 tbsp extra virgin olive oil

½ tsp salt

Peel the oranges with a sharp knife, taking care to remove all traces of the white pith. Slice the oranges horizontally into 6 or 7 slices.

Place these on an attractive serving plate.

Slice the fennel bulbs as thinly as possible and scatter the slices over the oranges.

Scatter the pomegranate arils over the orange and fennel slices.

To make the dressing, combine the ingredients and mix well so the honey dissolves and everything is mixed together.

Pour the dressing over the salad and scatter the mint to garnish.

Simple dishes are the best. This dish has three ingredients, plus seasoning. Choose a snug oven dish for baking the fennel so it stays nice and juicy and does not dry out. This dish makes a great entrée – or a simple supper dish . . . if you dare. I always think offering a single item makes everybody concentrate on the flavour. Take care with the cheese, too. Choose the very best gouda you can find for added flavour. We are lucky to have some excellent Dutch cheesemakers making traditional hard cheeses around the country.
A friend Angela Clifford who lives on a farm in North Canterbury suggested this recipe to me and she recommended the locally made Karikaas cheese from Rangiora.

Buttery braised fennel

SERVES 4–6
WINE SUGGESTION: CHARDONNAY
BEST IN SUMMER/AUTUMN

4 fennel bulbs

3 tbsp butter

salt and black pepper

150g gouda

Trim the fennel bulbs, discarding most of the feathery tops. Cut each into quarters lengthwise. It is important to retain the core so that the fennel stays intact and the segments do not split.

Put the fennel into a large saucepan and cover with hot salted water. Bring to a simmer and cook very gently until the fennel is almost soft (about 10 minutes, as you are parboiling it). Drain the fennel well.

Meanwhile heat the oven to 180°C. Generously butter an ovenproof gratin dish.

Lay the fennel pieces in the dish so they fit tightly together. Sprinkle with a few of the fennel leaves, roughly chopped, a little extra salt and plenty of freshly ground black pepper.

Finally grate the cheese and spread this evenly to cover the fennel.

Bake the dish in the oven until the top is golden and bubbly (about 20 minutes).

Serve as an entrée or with steak or chicken.

Many winter vegetables are often maligned as boring and tasteless, but they're usually the most versatile in our gardens. Cauliflower, an abundant crop of the cooler weather, is one such vegetable that has come into its own. I love the tightly curled head of creamy curds, surrounded by the pale green leaves, and its mild flavour. I'm also intrigued by the bright purple cauliflowers, and those lime-green pointed heads that can't seem to make up their minds whether they are cauli or broccoli. All varieties of cauliflower need to be eaten as freshly harvested as possible to retain their sweetness, with minimal cooking time.

Warm cauliflower salad

SERVES 4–6
WINE SUGGESTION: GRÜNER VELTLINER
BEST IN WINTER

1 cauliflower, cut into neat florets

2 cups baby spinach leaves

2 cheeks preserved lemon

150g soft feta cheese

100g hazelnuts, roasted

Dressing:

½ cup mint leaves, finely sliced

1 lemon, grated zest and juice

4 tbsp extra virgin lemon-infused olive oil

sea salt flakes to taste

pinch of sugar

Bring a large pan of salted water to the boil and plunge the cauliflower florets in. Simmer for about 5–6 minutes until the cauliflower is tender but still with a little bite.

While the cauliflower is cooking, wash the spinach leaves and keep aside. Discard the soft centres of the preserved lemon and finely dice the skin. Break the feta cheese into bite-sized nuggets. Roughly chop the roasted hazelnuts.

Combine all the dressing ingredients, tasting and adjusting the seasoning if necessary.

Drain the cauliflower and while still warm combine on a serving dish with the spinach, preserved lemon, feta cheese and hazelnuts.

Pour the dressing over and serve at once.

Always on the lookout for new recipe ideas, I am also a keen traveller. In a back street in Vienna, we came across a small Israeli café, Miznon, which may have been the most casually run place in the whole of that magnificently formal city. Food was served over the counter, from a small menu, and once diners had placed their order they were invited to help themselves to hummus, yogurt and flat bread from the sideboard while they waited. We ordered a whole roasted cauliflower, and it was absolutely magnificent. It was one of those occasions where I just could not wait to return home to try my hand at recreating the dish.

Roasted golden cauliflower

SERVES 4
WINE SUGGESTION: CHARDONNAY
BEST IN WINTER

1 medium cauliflower

4 tbsp extra virgin olive oil

½ tsp salt

½ tsp freshly ground black pepper

3 tbsp chopped mint leaves

To accompany:

6 tbsp thick Greek yogurt

4 tbsp freshly made hummus

extra olive oil

Preheat the oven to a moderate temperature, about 180°C.

Bring a large deep pan of slightly salted water to the boil.

Trim the cauliflower by slicing a little of the coarse base away, ensuring that the end of the core remains, to hold the cauliflower together. Keep a few of the fresher, more delicate leaves attached.

Plunge the cauliflower into the boiling water, turn down the heat and simmer gently for about 7–10 minutes until it is tender but not mushy. The fresher the cauliflower, the sweeter it will be.

Drain well and place snugly in a roasting pan. Drizzle with olive oil and roast for about 20 minutes or until golden brown. When ready to serve, pour over a little extra oil and scatter over black pepper and mint leaves.

To accompany the cauliflower, spoon the yogurt into a small bowl. Add the hummus on top of this and finish with some extra olive oil and mint. The mixture can be spooned over the cauliflower as it is eaten.

Serve hot or warm.

SECTION 2
Things to savour

54	Spring risotto with asparagus & broad beans
56	Mushroom risotto
58	Tomato & goat cheese tart
60	Baked aubergine, tomato & mozzarella
62	Japanese spring soba noodles
64	*Food Talk: Overcoming food waste*
66	Kumara gratin with horopito pepper
68	Pea, parsley, mint & feta fritters
70	Courgettes with spaghetti, basil & cheese
72	Spinach tart
74	Fig, blue cheese & bacon salad
76	Cabbage, bacon & potato soup
78	Crisp cheesy biscuits & cheese straws
80	Blue cheese & caramelised onion quiche
82	Cheesy cauliflower & leek bread pudding
84	Sausage, cavolo nero & fresh tomato pasta

Broad beans need to be picked while they are young and tender as fully developed beans become tough and require lengthy cooking. This versatile vegetable can be puréed or mashed, cloaked in a delicate sauce as a side dish for dinner or is super for adding to salads. Lemon, tarragon and a little garlic make perfect complementary flavours. Dealing with broad beans can be a chore. They must be removed from their pods by splitting them along the seam (expect to see between four and seven beans in each pod). The beans will have a pale grey/greenish skin that needs to be removed, unless they are small and young or the evergreen variety. Plunge them into boiling water and then into ice-cold water to stop the cooking process. The delicate inner bean can be released from its skin by gently squeezing it between the thumb and forefinger.

Spring risotto with asparagus & broad beans

SERVES 4
WINE SUGGESTION: SAUVIGNON BLANC
BEST IN SPRING

250g shelled broad beans

250g asparagus

200g fresh shelled peas (or frozen)

1.2 litres chicken or vegetable stock

60g butter

2 large shallots, peeled and finely chopped

200g arborio rice

100ml white wine

1 slice ham, cut into thin slithers

50g grated Grana Padano cheese

Remove the broad beans from their pods and place in a saucepan of boiling water for 30 seconds, then refresh under cold water. Remove the skins (see above). Discard the skins.

Cut the tips from the asparagus, snap the tough ends off, and plunge stalks and tips into boiling water, simmering for 2–3 minutes until just tender. Refresh under cold water.

Place the peas in a saucepan of boiling water and simmer for 2 minutes until tender.

Leave half the broad beans and asparagus tips aside. Purée the remaining broad beans, asparagus stalks and peas until smooth. Set aside.

Bring the stock in a saucepan to a slow simmer. Melt half the butter in another saucepan and add the shallots. Cook gently until the onion is translucent, then stir in the rice. Cook this for about 2–3 minutes, stirring constantly. Add the wine and turn the heat up. Ladle a little of the hot stock into the rice and stir well. As the liquid is absorbed, keep adding each ladleful of the hot stock, stirring constantly. When all the stock is absorbed and the rice is tender, stir in the green purée. Stir the ham and remaining butter through. Season to taste.

Steam the reserved asparagus tips and broad beans for 30 seconds. Place the risotto into four bowls and top with the asparagus tips and broad beans. Hand the cheese separately.

I always use my favourite enamelled Le Creuset cast-iron casserole dish for risotto and generally cook the rice without the usual technique of continually adding dollops of hot stock and constant stirring. Risotto can be tricky. Some cooks like their risotto rice cooked so each grain still has some 'bite', while I like the rice to reach the soft and fluffy stage. It's also a matter of taste either to serve risotto very 'sloppy' or to cook the rice a little longer so the texture of the dish is slightly stiffer and has dried out a little more. The heavy pan will hold the risotto's heat for a while but it will be necessary to poke holes in the rice to let air in and prevent the risotto from becoming gluggy.

Mushroom risotto

SERVES 4
WINE SUGGESTION: PINOT NOIR
BEST IN AUTUMN

10g dried porcini mushrooms

1 litre chicken or well-flavoured vegetable stock

2 tbsp olive oil

1 small onion finely chopped

1 clove garlic, crushed

2 large portabello mushrooms, cut into 1cm dice

pinch of nutmeg

350g Ferron carnaroli rice

2 tbsp butter

2 spring onions

6 white button mushrooms, finely sliced

2 tbsp freshly grated parmesan

3 tbsp finely chopped flat leafed parsley

Place the porcini mushrooms in a small bowl and cover with boiling water. Allow to soak for 15 minutes or more.

Put the stock in a pan and bring to a simmer.

Heat the olive oil in a heavy-based risotto or casserole dish and add the onion and garlic. Cook this over a gentle heat until it is turning golden brown. Drain the porcini, chop finely and add to the onion with the diced portabello mushrooms and grated nutmeg. Toss this over the heat until soft, then stir in the rice. Allow the rice to cook for a minute or two before stirring in a ladleful of the heated stock. Then tip in the rest of the stock at once, stirring well, until it reaches a simmer. Cover. Turn the heat as low as possible and allow the rice to cook for 14 minutes, stirring very occasionally. The rice should absorb almost all the stock and be tender.

Meanwhile, heat the butter in a small frying pan, add the spring onions and the sliced button mushrooms and sauté, stirring often until the mushrooms turn golden.

To finish, stir the parsley into the risotto, taste for salt and ladle generous portions onto four heated plates. Garnish each serving with the sautéed mushrooms and hand the grated parmesan separately.

This is a lovely, fragrant Mediterranean-inspired tart. Tarts are a stylish way to make an easy lunch or dinner dish. If you cannot get yellow tomatoes it will be equally delicious with ripe red tomatoes. My favourite pastry is the frozen flaky puff from Paneton, available in many supermarkets and specialist food stores.

Tomato & goat cheese tart

SERVES 6
WINE SUGGESTION: A FRUITY RIESLING
BEST IN SUMMER

250g puff pastry

2 tbsp Dijon-style mustard

500g large ripe tomatoes

salt and freshly ground pepper

pinch of sugar

100g soft goat cheese

2 tbsp chopped thyme

Roll the pastry out very thin and line a loose-bottomed 20–22cm tart tin, taking care to pull the pastry just over the rim of the tin. Prick the base of the pastry and refrigerate for an hour or more, so the pastry rests.

Preheat the oven to 200°C. Spread the mustard over the base, then slice the tomatoes very thickly and lay them in an overlapping pattern over the mustard. Sprinkle the salt, pepper and sugar over the tomatoes. Cut or break the goat cheese into small pieces and strew these over the tomatoes. Finally sprinkle the thyme leaves over the top.

Bake in the oven for 20 minutes or until the pastry is brown and crisp. Allow the tart to cool a little before serving as the tomatoes will be very hot. Serve with a crisp green salad.

A wonderfully satisfying oven-baked dish that can stand alone as dinner on a summer evening. Do not be tempted to miss out the step of precooking the aubergines, as this is the secret to the dish being so delicious. Be sure to find the light, white mozzarella for a perfect result. Fresh, authentic buffalo or cow mozzarella is packaged in a light brine and will only last two or three weeks in the refrigerator so use it generously.

Baked aubergine, tomato & mozzarella

SERVES 4
WINE SUGGESTION: A LIGHT, FRUITY RED WINE
BEST IN LATE SUMMER/AUTUMN

1 large aubergine

6 tbsp olive oil

salt and freshly ground black pepper

2 beefsteak tomatoes

1 large ball fresh mozzarella cheese

½ cup Italian-style tomato sauce (salsa or sugo)

a handful of basil leaves or oregano

freshly ground black pepper

Preheat the oven to 180°C.

Slice the aubergine into 10mm slices and score the surface of each slice with a sharp knife. Sprinkle with salt. Heat the olive oil in a large heavy-based frying pan, and when hot add the aubergine slices. Fry over gentle heat until golden, turning so both sides are coloured and the aubergine is soft. Remove from the heat to paper towels to drain.

Lay the cooked aubergine slices into a small ovenproof dish, covering the base evenly. Slice the tomatoes and lay these on top of the aubergine.

Cut the mozzarella into thin slices and cover the tomatoes to form another layer. Pour over the tomato sauce and add the basil or oregano, with a little black pepper.

Bake in the oven for 15–20 minutes or until the dish is sizzling. Serve as an entrée or as an accompaniment to grilled chicken or lamb.

This simple soba noodle dish is dressed with miso, the flavoursome paste that is one of the most important building blocks of Japanese cuisine. A key ingredient in miso soup and other dressings, marinades and dishes, it will keep for months in an airtight jar if refrigerated. I was inspired to make this soba noodle recipe after a spring-time visit to Tokyo. The legendary cherry blossoms were in full bloom and almost every dish we ate was light and colourful, celebrating the coming of spring. Japanese cuisine is all about the seasons!

Japanese spring soba noodles

SERVES 4 AS A SIDE DISH OR TWO AS A MAIN COURSE
WINE SUGGESTION: DRY GEWÜRZTRAMINER
BEST IN SPRING

For the miso dressing:

2 tbsp organic miso

2 tbsp rice vinegar

4 tbsp grapeseed oil

1 tsp runny honey

For the noodles:

200g baby mushrooms

2 tbsp vegetable oil (grapeseed or rice bran)

12 baby carrots

1 cup broccoli sprouts

180g soba noodles

shreds of Japanese pickled ginger

sesame seeds, lightly toasted in a dry frying pan

coriander or Vietnamese mint leaves for garnish

Prepare the dressing by mixing the miso, vinegar, oil and honey together in a jar and shake or stir until all dissolved.

To prepare the vegetables, slice the mushrooms as thinly as possible. Heat the oil in a frying pan and add the mushrooms. Toss them over gentle heat for 2–3 minutes until they begin to wilt but do not let them become soft and mushy. Remove, then add the carrots to the frying pan. You may need to add some extra oil to pan-roast the carrots over a gentle heat until tender, tossing frequently.

Simmer a pan of salted water and blanch the broccoli sprouts for 2 minutes. Drain.

Meanwhile bring another pan of salted water to the boil and plunge the soba noodles into the water. Simmer for 3–4 minutes until soft and pliable. Drain well and toss in a little sesame oil so they don't get sticky.

To assemble the dish, toss the noodles (either warm or cold) in half the miso dressing. Place on a large serving platter and top with the mushrooms, carrots and broccoli. Drizzle over the remaining dressing and garnish with pickled ginger, sesame seeds and the herb leaves.

Food Talk //
Overcoming food waste

One of the trending topics on the culinary scene that really concerns me is food waste. Researchers tell us that every day the amount of food thrown away would be more than enough to feed every starving child on the planet. It is a scandal that too much food is unfairly distributed, discarded when still edible, or simply bought and not consumed.

Farmers take pride in growing and producing food, and food cultures need to be respectful of food. Right now we are witnessing a sea change in the thinking about waste and the management of food. Around the country volunteers stand by to gather surplus food from supermarkets, and businesses use ingenious or obvious methods to redistribute it. Some food goes directly to needy folk, while others create secondary products from the surplus that can be sold commercially. The social conscience towards food distribution is on the rise and we all benefit from anything that alleviates hunger and repurposes food.

Despite supermarket chains' recent efforts to address food waste, the biggest culprits are often us, the consumers, who cook in our home kitchens. It can be the result of sloppy shopping – buying and cooking more food than is needed in one meal, leftover food too often destined for the bin, and yet another meal cooked from scratch with fresh ingredients.

A few years back I was quoted about what's in my freezer, where I said: 'I only keep ice cream, frozen peas and ice for gin and tonic.' Times have changed. I now think more carefully about not disposing of leftovers, and I package up anything that's useful, sealing and labelling the food. These leftovers can form the basis of a jolly good meal or a delicious stock.

Leftover rice and unwanted bread are possibly the most discarded ingredients in New Zealand kitchens. With rice, I believe too many cooks can hardly believe a small cup or two of rice grains will swell up to such a quantity when cooked. There are numerous ways to use that leftover cooked rice, as it freezes beautifully. Remember, bacteria spores can germinate and produce a toxin that causes food poisoning if the rice is left for any lengthy period at room temperature. Cool it rapidly and refrigerate the leftover rice as soon as possible, leaving it there for no more than a day, or pack into an airtight bag and freeze it. It can then be flavoured with herbs and spices, added to mince for pie fillings or meatballs, used to bulk out stuffing, added to a casserole or curry, made into savoury rice balls, a sweet rice pudding with fruit and cream, or a filling for omelettes and pancakes.

Stale bread has myriad uses, too. The easiest is to turn it into crumbs to have on standby in the freezer. If the bread is a couple of days old, lightly brush it with water and pop it into a preheated moderate oven for 15 minutes or less, depending on how thick your loaf is. It will emerge hot and fragrant with a crisp exterior. Or you can slice the loaf thinly and bake it into crisp bread sticks to take the place of crackers or chips. Thinly sliced leftover bread make terrific little savoury cases to serve with fillings as a snack. Butter the bread and push the slices into a muffin pan to bake in a moderate oven until crisp. Use the leftover bread in a bread-and-butter pudding, a summer pudding with berries, or the glorious cheesy cauliflower and leek bread pudding recipe you will find in this section.

Here are other easy recipes to use up those leftovers:

Bacon and egg fried rice

4 tbsp vegetable oil

1 small onion, finely sliced

2 cloves garlic, crushed

4 rashers bacon, cut into 5cm strips

2 cups cooked leftover rice

1 tsp soy sauce

½ tsp freshly ground black pepper

4 eggs

4 tbsp finely chopped parsley

Heat 2 tablespoons of the oil in a large, heavy saucepan. Add the onion and garlic and cook over low to medium heat until the onion softens. Take care the onion does not get too brown as it will spoil the taste of the dish. Add the bacon and cook this with the onion, stirring so it becomes golden but does not burn. When the onion and bacon are cooked, add the rice to the pan. Toss continuously, adding the soy sauce to flavour along with some water or stock if the rice becomes a little dry. Toss the parsley into the rice and season with salt and pepper to taste. Leave the pan on a low heat while you cook the eggs. Heat the remaining oil in a frying pan. Once hot, tip the eggs in one at a time, evenly spaced. Using a spoon or fork, gently draw the edge of each egg in, so it does not spread widely. (Fresher eggs will not spread out much.) Remove the egg when the white is just cooked, and the yolk has set. Do not flip the egg. Spoon out the rice, dividing it between four heated plates and place one egg on the top of each pile of rice. Serve at once with spicy Sriracha or pepper sauce.

Serves 4 for a morning-after breakfast or brunch

Perfect crumbed food

4 tbsp white flour

1 egg

½ tsp salt

freshly ground black pepper

1 cup sourdough breadcrumbs

For frying:

4 tbsp light odourless oil (rice bran or grapeseed)

1 tbsp butter

You need to assemble a working line of the ingredients so you can freshly crumb your food immediately before frying it. Place the flour on a shallow plate. Next to this, place a bowl in which you have beaten the egg with the salt and pepper to season it. After the bowl, you need another shallow bowl with the breadcrumbs. Heat the frying pan, add the oil and butter and you're ready to go. Dust the food you are cooking (fish, schnitzel, fishcakes, croquettes, etc) with the flour and shake any excess off. Dip the floured food into the egg so it is completely coated and then dip the egg-covered food into the crumbs, making sure every surface is coated. Slide the crumbed food into the frying pan over a gentle heat and cook, turning once, until both sides are golden and the food is cooked through. Drain on kitchen paper before serving while still hot.

Monique Fiso, a young Māori chef whom I met when she first returned to New Zealand after cooking in New York City, is now leading the way in reconnecting Māori food to New Zealanders and reinventing food traditions by giving them her own classy twist. She is an inspiration to me with her edgy ideas and brilliant food. We discussed Matariki, the festivities of Māori New Year, and she said she always serves a kumara dish at the celebratory feast. Fiso suggested making the kumara into a creamy gratin, 'as everything tastes better with cream and butter'. I agree and this is my take on her idea.

Kumara gratin with horopito pepper

SERVES 6
WINE SUGGESTION: PINOT NOIR
BEST IN ANY SEASON

2 tbsp butter

200ml milk

300ml cream

1 bay leaf

salt & black pepper

1.5kg red-skinned kumara

2 pinches horopito pepper

50g parmesan cheese

Preheat the oven to 200°C. Butter an ovenproof dish, around 30cm x 20cm x 6cm.

Bring the milk, cream and bay leaf to the boil in a saucepan. Simmer for a few minutes, then remove from heat and season with salt and pepper.

Finely slice the kumara and layer this in the gratin dish. Cover with the hot cream and horopito and shake to evenly distribute the liquid. Sprinkle with parmesan, cover with tinfoil and bake for 50 minutes or until the kumara are tender when a skewer is pushed into them.

I love to whip fritters up if we are sharing a glass of wine with friends. I think of them as beautiful blotting paper, and it's always good to offer something substantial to eat when serving alcohol. Peas and mint are natural partners and combine beautifully in this fritter recipe with the help of some sharp feta cheese. You could exchange the peas for other green vegetables: broccoli, finely sliced beans, chopped fennel, grated courgettes or finely sliced asparagus.

Pea, parsley, mint & feta fritters

SERVES 6
WINE SUGGESTION: OAK-AGED OR WILD-FERMENT SAUVIGNON BLANC
BEST IN SPRING AND SUMMER

1 shallot, finely chopped

1 tsp butter

250g baby peas, thawed

½ cup roughly chopped parsley and mint

3 eggs

2 tbsp flour

1 tsp baking powder

100g crumbly feta

salt and freshly ground black pepper to taste

4 tbsp grapeseed or other vegetable oil

To serve: ¼ cup spicy chutney

Place the chopped shallot with the butter in a microwave-safe dish. Cook for two minutes on high until the shallot is softened and translucent. This can also be done in a frying pan over gentle heat.

Tip the cooked shallot into a food processor with the peas, parsley and mint and pulse until the mixture is almost smooth. Add the eggs, process again, and then add the flour and baking powder and pulse a couple of times to incorporate everything. Tip this mixture into a bowl, crumble the feta in and mix very gently so small lumps of feta remain. Taste the mixture and season with black pepper, adding extra salt if needed, although watch carefully as feta can be very salty.

Note: If you do not have a food processor or blender you can mash the peas, finely chop the herbs and stir everything together really well. The resulting fritters will be a little chunkier but just as delicious.

To cook, heat 2 tablespoons of the oil in a frying pan until it is quite hot. Add tablespoons of the pea mixture, turn down the heat and cook gently on both sides for 3–4 minutes each side or until the fritters are just firm to the touch. Cook in batches of four or five at a time, adding extra oil to the pan as needed between batches.

Makes about 15–16 fritters. Serve on a platter, with a side of spicy chutney to dab on the fritters.

Courgettes (zucchini) are a vegetable that are either embraced or disdained, and never much in between. Choose young, firm, glossy courgettes and you will not need to peel them. And never boil or simmer this vegetable as it will become soggy and mushy and have none of the texture that makes it interesting eating. One of my favourite ways to cook courgettes is to slice them thickly and toss them into a pan with butter or a light olive oil flavoured with a pinch of ground cumin and plenty of salt and pepper. Toss them well over the heat until they just start to soften and then remove from the heat. Add a little extra squirt of lemon juice and eat them right away. If I am cooking on the barbecue or on a cast-iron ridged grill pan, I cut the courgettes in half, lengthwise, toss them in olive oil, salt and some freshly chopped herbs like dill or basil and cook over a medium heat until they are still crunchy in the middle but softening on the outside.

Courgettes with spaghetti, basil & cheese

SERVES 4
WINE SUGGESTION: PINOT NOIR
BEST IN SUMMER

4 courgettes

1 tbsp ground cumin

1 lemon

salt and pepper to season

4 tbsp extra virgin olive oil

150g spaghetti

50g parmesan cheese

a handful of fresh basil leaves

Slice the courgettes into thin, even rounds. Dust the slices with cumin, the grated zest of the lemon and salt and pepper. Heat three tablespoons of olive oil in a frying pan, and add the courgette slices, tossing occasionally until they are golden and beginning to soften.

Meanwhile bring a large pot of salted water to the boil and cook the spaghetti, according to the time given on the packet or until it is tender. When it is cooked, drain the spaghetti well and return to the pan with an extra tablespoon of olive oil and the juice of the lemon. Toss this over the heat for a few seconds to coat the spaghetti strands.

To serve, pile the spaghetti into four pasta bowls. Divide the courgettes into four portions, and toss these onto the spaghetti. Add the grated cheese and basil leaves with an extra grind of black pepper and serve at once.

Spinach can be easily spoilt in two ways. Firstly, always wash your spinach well, as this is one vegetable that can harbour the particles of earth it was plucked from. Let the spinach soak for thirty minutes in cold water before running the leaves under the tap. Secondly, drain cooked spinach very well. Best way is to place it between two plates and push hard together so all the water runs away.

Spinach tart

SERVES 6
WINE SUGGESTION: PINOT GRIS
BEST IN AUTUMN/WINTER

For the pastry:

150g chilled butter

200g flour

pinch of salt

¼ cup ice-cold water

For the filling:

750g baby spinach leaves

30g butter

salt and pepper

75g ricotta cheese

30g grated parmesan cheese

120ml thick cream

2 large eggs, beaten

a pinch of ground nutmeg

To make the pastry, chop the butter into small pieces and place in the food processor with the flour and salt. Pulse this together until the butter is incorporated. Slowly add the water through the feed tube, pulsing the pastry until the mixture resembles coarse crumbs. Turn out onto a clean surface and lightly knead to form a ball. Chill the pastry for 30 minutes before rolling out on a floured board to fit a 20–22cm flan tin, or a rectangular 12 x 30cm tin. Rest this pastry case for at least 30 minutes.

To bake the case 'blind', scrunch up baking paper then smooth it over the pastry, right into the corners. Fill with baking beads or rice and bake for 10–15 minutes at 200°C. Take the case from the oven and when cooled, remove the beads and paper.

To make the filling, wash and drain the spinach well, removing any thick stalks. Melt the butter in a saucepan and cook the spinach gently with a pinch of salt until wilted. Drain well, squeezing it out to lose almost all the moisture. Chop the spinach finely. Season to taste with pepper and more salt if needed.

Blend the ricotta and parmesan in a bowl, then beat in the cream and eggs and nutmeg. Fold the spinach into this mixture and spoon into the baked pastry case. Bake the tart in a moderate oven for 25 minutes or until the mixture has just set but is still a little wobbly. Serve with sliced tomatoes.

In late summer when fresh figs are abundant, this salad will be very welcome. There's something wonderful about the combination of sweet tender figs and savoury, creamy blue cheese that will win over even the most reluctant blue-cheese eater.

Fig, blue cheese & bacon salad

SERVES 4 AS AN ENTRÉE
WINE SUGGESTION: DRY PINOT GRIS
BEST IN AUTUMN

Dressing:

2 cheeks preserved lemons, diced

1 lemon, juice only

freshly ground black pepper

5 tbsp grapeseed oil

Salad:

6 ripe figs

150g soft blue cheese

6 rashers streaky bacon

2 handfuls wild rocket leaves

¼ cup roasted almonds

2 tbsp Italian parsley, chopped

Make the dressing by shaking all the ingredients together in a small jar.

To make the salad, wash the figs and cut each into half. Break the cheese into small chunks.

Turn on the grill and while it is heating, cut each piece of bacon in two. Place the bacon under the heat and grill until the bacon is golden and crisp.

Arrange the washed rocket leaves on a serving platter. Nestle the figs into the leaves and scatter the blue cheese and almonds around. Top with the bacon while still hot and spoon the dressing over with the parsley. Serve at once.

Cabbage is an unsung hero of the food world. When it's fresh and crisp it makes a great base to build on for all sorts of tasty dishes. Make sure you find a smoked bacon for this chunky warming soup as the smoky flavour will make the soup wonderfully appetising.

Cabbage, bacon & potato soup

SERVES 4–6
WINE SUGGESTION: CHARDONNAY
BEST IN WINTER

1 tbsp butter

150g smoky bacon, cut into strips

1 large onion, peeled and finely diced

8 baby red jacket potatoes, thinly sliced

1.5 litres chicken stock

salt and freshly ground pepper

¼ cabbage, finely sliced

2 tbsp chervil, chopped or sprigs

Melt the butter in a large heavy pan, add the bacon and fry for a minute or two. Add the onion and cook over a gentle heat until the onion is soft and sweet, stirring frequently. Add the potatoes and the stock. Allow to simmer very slowly for 20 minutes. Add the cabbage with seasoning and simmer for 5 minutes. Finally add the chervil and serve in heated bowls with crusty bread.

These cheesy biscuits are ideal for whipping up to serve with cheese, or to give as a gift when you are invited for drinks or dinner. Be sure to use authentic parmesan, but if you find imported Parmigiana Reggiano is too expensive, do a taste test on whichever substitute you use. The flavour of the cheese intensifies in the baking process.

Crisp cheesy biscuits

MAKES 36
WINE SUGGESTION: CHAMPAGNE

100g cold unsalted butter, cut into chunks

100g plain flour, plus a little extra

pinch salt

½ tsp mustard powder

50g finely grated tasty cheddar

50g finely grated parmesan

1 egg

extra cheese and caraway seeds for decoration

Preheat the oven to 180°C.

Put the butter and flour into a food processor with the mustard powder, salt and cheese. Pulse the mixture in short spurts until it forms a ball. Stop the machine immediately, turn out and wrap in cling film. Chill in the fridge for at least 30 minutes.

Lightly flour a clean work top and gently roll out the pastry to about 1cm thickness. Using a pastry cutter, cut into 5cm rounds. Lay them on a greased baking tray or a tray lined with baking paper.

Beat the egg and brush the surface of each biscuit, sprinkling over extra grated parmesan or a few caraway seeds. Bake for 15 minutes or until golden brown and crisp.

Place the biscuits on a rack to cool. They will keep well for 3 to 4 days in a sealed container.

Cheese straws

MAKES ABOUT 15
BEST IN ANY SEASON

250g puff pastry or trimmings

1 egg white

100g parmesan cheese, finely grated

100g sharp cheddar cheese, finely grated

pinch of cayenne

Preheat the oven to 200°C.

Roll the pastry into a large rectangle on a clean, floured bench top. Brush the lower half of the pastry with beaten egg white. Mix the cheeses together with the cayenne. Divide this mixture in half and put one lot aside. Sprinkle the other half over the egg white, then fold the upper half of the pastry down onto the cheese. Using a little extra flour, seal the edges by pressing down with the rolling pin, then roll this pastry 'sandwich' out to the original size of the pastry. Brush the entire sheet of pastry with the egg white and sprinkle over the reserved cheese mixture. Chill for about 15 minutes, then cut into thin strips of 1–2 cm. Twist these into straws and lay on a baking tray.

Bake for 10–15 minutes until golden brown and cooked through. Cool on a wire rack and eat the same day.

One of the joys of the New Zealand food scene is seeing the part that our producers play in contributing diverse products to our culinary landscape. Whether they're artisans, corporate producers or the farmers who supply raw product direct from the land, they all influence the food that we eat here or export around the world. I was privileged to be the head judge for the inaugural Outstanding NZ Food Producer Awards 2017. Even though my food-writing career has been dedicated to and inspired by our fabulous food, I was still stunned by the ingenuity and quality of the entries. So much so that I created this tart using three of the winning products: Paneton pastry, Jersey Girl milk and Whitestone Windsor blue cheese.

Blue cheese & caramelised onion quiche

SERVES 4
WINE SUGGESTION: SAUVIGNON BLANC
BEST IN ANY SEASON

500g ready rolled puff pastry

2 large onions

50g butter

pinch each of salt, black pepper and sugar

2 tbsp red wine vinegar

100g mascarpone

3 egg yolks

200ml full cream milk

200g blue cheese

Preheat the oven to 190°C. Line the puff pastry into a 20cm loose-bottomed quiche or tart tin, approximately 30 x 12cm. Prick the base of the pastry, cover with crushed baking paper and add some baking beads or rice to hold the paper down. Stand for about 20 minutes then pop the tart shell into the heated oven and bake for 15 minutes. Set aside to cool.

Slice the onions finely. Heat the butter in a small pan and when it starts to foam, toss in the onions with the salt, pepper and sugar. Cook over gentle heat so they become soft and eventually turn golden. After about 30 minutes add the vinegar and allow this to become absorbed. Set aside to cool.

Beat the mascarpone, eggs and milk together until smooth, then crumble the blue cheese into the mixture with a little extra salt and pepper.

Spread the onion mixture over the base of the prepared tart shell. Pour in the cheesy mixture and bake for about 20–25 minutes until firm and the pastry has become golden and crisp. Serve with sliced fresh tomatoes.

Everybody loves the sort of food that is a one-pot meal, filled with robust flavours and textures, and often prepared ahead. This dish, which proved to be an all-time *Listener* favourite is like that. It's easy to eat with a fork, so friends and family can be cosily settled by the fire, plate in hand, with an accompanying glass or two of red wine to enjoy. The eggy custard puffs up in the oven, and with its crisp buttery top it's the ultimate comfort food. If you want to serve it for eight people just double the quantities and choose a much larger dish. The vegetables can be prepared ahead, and the custard ingredients measured out but not beaten together, until you are ready to bake the dish.

Cheesy cauliflower & leek bread pudding

SERVES 4
WINE SUGGESTION: FRUITY CHARDONNAY
BEST IN AUTUMN/WINTER

1 large leek

50g butter

200g baby spinach leaves, washed

½ cauliflower, cut into small florets

4 large eggs

200ml milk

150ml cream

75g grated tasty gouda cheese

½ cup crumbled feta cheese

2 tsp thyme leaves, finely chopped

pinch of freshly grated nutmeg

salt and freshly ground black pepper

4 thick slices sourdough bread, crusts removed

Butter an ovenproof casserole or soufflé dish. Preheat the oven to 170°C.

Slice the leek finely. Melt the butter in a wide saucepan over gentle heat, add the leek and cook for 5 minutes until it softens without browning. Add the spinach leaves and toss over the heat until they wilt. Continue to cook for a minute or two so any juices evaporate. Set this aside.

Meanwhile bring salted water to the boil and blanch the cauliflower for 2 minutes. Drain well and add to the leeks and spinach.

Place the eggs, milk and cream in a large bowl and whisk together. Add half the grated cheese, the feta, thyme, nutmeg and salt and pepper to taste and mix well.

Cut the bread into large cubes and fold into the egg mixture with the reserved vegetables. Tip everything into the prepared dish, and scatter over the remaining cheese. Allow the dish to sit for about ten minutes so the bread absorbs some of the custard. Bake for about 45 minutes, until it is puffed and golden and still a little moist in the centre.

Serve immediately with a green salad.

We all love pasta, but good-quality Italian artisan pasta is made from hard durum wheat, which is preferred for its colour and cooking ability. The pasta shapes are made by extruding the pasta dough through bronze mills or dies, which gives the pasta a rougher, porous surface. Connoisseurs appreciate this as the slight inconsistencies allow the pasta to soak up the sauce. But which shape do you choose? Pasta comes in about 350 different shapes, each with a tale to be told. Regions of Italy (and France and Spain) have their own specialties, just as they have sauces. General rules are tubular shapes suit hearty, thick sauces like bolognese and ragu, as they capture the sauce. Linguine, pappardelle and other wide, flat pastas are excellent to sop up creamy sauce. Thin, long pasta such as spaghetti and spaghettini is best with thin tomato and olive oil sauces. And really chunky sauce with sausage and pieces of hearty vegetable like I used for this recipe will be excellent with rustic pasta shapes.

Sausage, cavolo nero & fresh tomato pasta

SERVES 4
WINE SUGGESTION: PINOT NOIR
BEST IN ANY SEASON

400g pork and fennel sausage

30ml extra virgin olive oil

1 white onion, finely chopped

2 cloves garlic, crushed

½ cup white wine

1 large fresh tomato, chopped

6 leaves cavolo nero, finely sliced

400g pasta (orecchiette, cavalini, cavatelli or similar)

100g pecorino, shaved into very thin slices

freshly ground black pepper

Split the skins down the length of the sausages. Remove the sausage meat, discarding the skin.

Heat the oil in a heavy pan. Add the onion, cook for 2–3 minutes, then crumble the sausage meat into the oil and onion and stir with a wooden spoon to break the meat up. Cook until turning golden brown, stirring often.

Add the garlic, the wine and the tomato. Bring to a simmer, add the sliced cavolo nero and cook for about 15 minutes over low heat.

Meanwhile bring a large pan of salted water to the boil and add the pasta. Cook until tender or according to the packet instructions.

Drain the pasta once it is cooked, keeping about half a cup of the cooking liquid. Tip the pasta into the pan with the sausage sauce, adding a little of the reserved cooking water. Leave over low heat for about 5 minutes, so the pasta absorbs the flavours of the sauce.

To serve, divide the pasta between 4 heated plates, and finish with freshly ground black pepper and top with shavings of pecorino.

SECTION 3
Something fishy

88	Whitebait fritters
90	Salmon in a spring vegetable broth
92	Kingfish carpaccio
94	Hāpuku, shiitake & asparagus stir-fry
96	*Food Talk: A sustainable seafood supply*
98	Avocado & gin-and-lime cured salmon
100	Gurnard ceviche with melon & seaweed
102	Kahawai ceviche with radishes, beetroot & avocado
104	Portuguese-style clam stew
106	Creamy oyster & leek soup
108	Fresh salmon with yuzu oil & garden herbs
110	Turmeric & lime fish fillets
112	Oyster & chive frittata
114	Salmon coulibiac
116	Clams with corn & chilli
118	Salmon & cucumber green curry
120	Mussel & salmon chowder

Native whitebait, the tiny little fish that almost could swim through the eye of a needle, is a uniquely New Zealand food. It's delicate, seasonal and always a hit. Recently there's been discussion around the sustainability of the catch since it's not subject to controlled quotas like other fish. The good news is an enterprising business, Manāki, is raising whitebait at an aquaculture installation in Warkworth, north of Auckland. Despite some fancy ideas dreamed up by innovative chefs, these tasty fish are traditionally served in fritters. I believe the best fritters are devoid of flour and excess seasoning – just plenty of whitebait, bound with a fresh free-range egg and a pinch of salt, and served with wedges of fresh lemon.

Whitebait fritters

MAKES ABOUT 15
WINE SUGGESTION: SAUVIGNON BLANC
BEST IN SPRING

2 fresh organic eggs

200g whitebait

sea salt flakes

freshly ground black pepper

2 tbsp oil

2 tbsp fresh butter

lemon wedges to serve

Beat the eggs in a bowl until they are light and frothy. Add the whitebait with a generous pinch of salt and plenty of fresh pepper. Mix well.

Heat the oil and butter together in a large frying pan over medium heat. When the butter starts to bubble and spit, add even tablespoons of the egg and whitebait mixture (about 5–6 at a time) and cook for 1–2 minutes, then flip each fritter over and cook the other side. Immediately remove to a warmed plate. Continue cooking in batches of about 5 fritters until the mixture is finished. Serve at once with fresh lemon wedges, as finger food or as an entrée for 4 people.

The arrival of spring heralds the most exciting season in the kitchen; there's no other time in the year when fresh food from the garden seems quite as fresh and inviting. This recipe is a celebration of spring vegetables – the first of the new potatoes, asparagus and broad beans. The centrepiece is fresh salmon, which is also at its best as the weather warms up after the winter.

Salmon in a spring vegetable broth

SERVES 4
WINE MATCH: A LIGHTER CHARDONNAY
BEST IN SPRING

4 x 150g pieces fresh salmon

sea salt

2 cups baby new potatoes, scrubbed

8 spears of fresh asparagus, cut into 6cm lengths

1 cup broad beans, blanched and skinned

20 sugar snap peas

1 cup fish or vegetable stock

2 tbsp cream

2 tbsp butter

2 tbsp olive oil

1 cup baby watercress

Trim the salmon if necessary and sprinkle with a little sea salt. Keep aside while you prepare the vegetables.

Bring a pan of salted water to the boil, add the potatoes and cook until tender. This should take about 10–12 minutes. While the potatoes are cooking, steam the asparagus, broad beans and sugar snap peas for 2 minutes.

To make the sauce, place the stock in a small pan and reduce by two-thirds. Add the cream, bring to a boil and add the butter. Stir well then remove from the heat.

Heat a frying pan and add the olive oil. When it is hot add the salmon, skin side down and cover the pan with a lid or some foil. Cook the salmon gently for about 3 minutes.

To serve, place each piece of salmon on a heated plate, and share the vegetables, including the drained potatoes, equally. Pour over the sauce and top each piece of salmon with a tangle of watercress.

This is a favourite of mine that I often prepare to take if invited to summer drinks. I always make this when I have fresh fish that my husband catches. I can whip this up in a matter of minutes and it's always a hit, even with folk who have not tried raw fish before. The fish only needs to marinate for about ten minutes. If you cannot get kingfish this will also work well with tuna or swordfish but it's important to have a firm-fleshed fish. All the ingredients should be fresh as fresh, and feel free to substitute coriander or mint for a slightly different flavour. The pink peppercorns are unusual but add nuttiness and surprising sweetness to the fish.

Kingfish carpaccio

SERVES 4–6
WINE SUGGESTION: SAUVIGNON BLANC
BEST IN SPRING/SUMMER

200g fresh kingfish fillet in one piece

3 tbsp extra virgin olive oil

juice and zest of 1 large lemon, finely grated

2 tsp dried pink peppercorns

1 tbsp finely chopped parsley

salt and freshly ground black pepper

Choose a large flat serving plate.

Ensure the fish is straight from the fridge as it must be cold to be sliced very thinly. Using a sharp thin-bladed knife, cut the fish as thinly as possible, laying out each slice on the plate as you go. Slightly overlap each slice as the fish needs to be able to absorb the dressing.

Drizzle with the olive oil and lemon juice so each piece is well coated.

Grate a little lemon zest over, scatter the peppercorns and herbs and finish with a liberal sprinkling of salt and freshly ground black pepper.

To serve, hand out small forks or chopsticks to lift the slices of fish off the platter to eat while enjoying a cool drink.

Hāpuku is the most popular fish cooked in our kitchen. Even though my husband is a recreational fisherman and tends to come home with a catch that might include kahawai, gurnard, snapper and the occasional northerly blue cod, it is hāpuku (or grouper) that we love the most for its thick, meaty flesh. This dish is lovely in spring when asparagus is bountiful, but in other seasons you could substitute beans or broccoli.

Hāpuku, shiitake & asparagus stir-fry

SERVES 2
WINE SUGGESTION: PINOT GRIS
BEST IN SPRING

200g shiitake mushrooms

250g asparagus spears

2 spring onions

2 tbsp soy sauce

1 tbsp lemon juice

1 tsp honey

½ tsp black pepper

2 tbsp peanut or grapeseed oil

½ cup chicken stock or water

300g hāpuku (or John Dory)

Prepare all the ingredients before you begin to cook.

Trim the woody stalks from the shiitake and slice into 2cm pieces. Snap the woody ends from the asparagus spears and peel the lower part of any thick stalks. Chop the spring onions into 1cm pieces.

Mix the soy sauce, lemon juice and honey together.

Slice the fish into 2cm thick nuggets.

Heat the oil in a wok until almost smoking, then toss in the onions and mushrooms. Toss over the heat for about two minutes then add the asparagus. Continue to toss over high heat for a minute or two longer.

Add the stock or water. Allow the vegetables to continue to cook over the high heat, stirring occasionally until almost all the liquid has evaporated and the vegetables are tender and still a little crisp. This should take about 4 minutes.

Add the soy sauce mixture, toss through really well and finally add the fish. Allow the fish to cook until it starts to turn opaque, moving it around very gently so it does not break up. Season with the black pepper and serve at once with boiled rice or noodles.

Food Talk //
A sustainable seafood supply

When it comes to seafood I am committed to finding fish from a sustainable catch. My husband, Murray, is a recreational fisherman who keeps to the law when he's out fishing. There's a fishing chart by the boat ramp where he launches Rain Dear, his little fishing boat he named after me. Murray chases after the kingfish, gurnard and snapper that predominate locally, yet I am overjoyed when he brings home kahawai or other more wild fish. The versatile kahawai might be my favourite fish. Too many people think of it as a bait fish, but I love it fresh and raw as sashimi, or pan-fried in a little butter with herbs and lemon. And it is luscious smoked and eaten warm, directly from the smoker, with mānuka sawdust to add another layer of flavour.

I have great respect for the New Zealand commercial fishing quota system. Our fishing industry has its local critics but it is a world-leading system with many checks and balances to ensure all fish offered for sale, for export, or used in commercial food production is continually monitored. I always look for wild catch or long-line caught fish.

Supermarkets and fishmongers will only change direction when there's customer pressure on them for lesser-known fish, so never be afraid to ask for wild-caught kahawai, lemon fish, mullet, hoki and a host of other species rarely stocked. (And try to find fish with the skin still attached. The skin is delicious!) We need to keep thinking about the sustainability of the fish schools in our oceans.

Our total New Zealand coastline measures almost 20,000 kilometres and this includes inlets and the coast that circles our offshore islands, which provides a haven for aquaculture. Sustainably managed, aquaculture provides a bright future as the ocean's bounty diminishes and some species are in danger of disappearing. Presently, the New Zealand aquaculture industry grows salmon, mussels, and oysters that earn export dollars, and a whitebait business addressing the claims that it is unsustainable. It's my belief that good science will provide us with fish and seafood for many generations to come.

A word about selecting and buying fresh fish: Look carefully at the fish you are offered. It should be bright and appear moist. If the fish is whole, the eyes should be bright and shiny, not sullen and sunken. Do not be afraid to ask to smell the fish as old fish carries a strong smell, almost like ammonia. If you intend to make a ceviche or another marinated raw fish dish it is imperative to find sparkling fresh fish.

Hopefully your fish will be packed in a foil bag to keep it cool as you transport it home. Once home, remove the fish from its wrapping, place on a plate and cover it loosely with waxed paper or foil. Try to cook it within a few hours. If you plan to eat it within a day or two, put your fish in a Ziploc bag, press all the air our and lay the bag on ice in the refrigerator to keep it as cold as possible. And do not shy away from purchasing frozen fish. Most often it will be frozen immediately when caught to retain the freshness, so as long as it has been caught within the past few weeks, it will be every bit as good as the fresh fish my husband brings home.

A FEW TIPS FOR PAN-FRYING FISH

- If possible use a non-stick frying pan and a non-stick spatula or fish slice.

- Pat the fish dry with a kitchen paper towel.

- Season the fish with salt (and pepper if you want) just before cooking it. Do not season ahead of time as the salt will draw out moisture from the fish.

- Dust the fish with a very light coat of flour which helps to keep the interior of the fish moist.

- Place the frying pan on the stove top over medium heat and add a flavourless oil. When the oil is almost starting to smoke, add a knob of butter and let that melt. Put the fish in the pan, and the heat should immediately seal the fish and crisp the surface. Do not overcrowd the pan, even if it means cooking your fish in batches.

- Cook for about 90 seconds to 2 minutes on the first side, depending on the thickness of your fish, then turn it over and cook for a further 90 seconds to 2 minutes. It should be firm and slightly springy to the touch.

- Remove the fish from the pan and place on a plate lined with a paper towel to absorb any excess fat.

- Serve immediately, so have all your vegetables or salad ready before you even start cooking the fish.

Another joy of spring produce is the arrival of the new season's avocados, when we can purchase them in abundance again, with prices dropping to an affordable level. It always amuses me when people groan about the price when trying to buy them out of season. I guess we still have a way to go in educating that the prime seasonal fare is usually when prices are at their lowest. Avocados are extremely versatile. The texture of a just-ripe avocado is perfect to add to salads and sandwiches, as in this recipe. Always treat the avocado with respect and nothing more than the gentlest handling to avoid bruising and creating dark marks in the flesh. It is important to purchase the freshest salmon possible for this sophisticated salad recipe.

Avocado & gin-and-lime cured salmon

SERVES 4
WINE SUGGESTION: SAUVIGNON BLANC
BEST IN SPRING/SUMMER

300g fresh salmon fillet, skin on, pin-boned

2 tsp sea salt

1 tsp caster sugar

1 lime, juice and grated zest

4 tbsp gin

2 avocados

1 small fennel bulb, thinly sliced

1 cup watercress

1 tbsp extra virgin olive oil

salt and freshly ground black pepper

For the garnish: 1 extra lime, very thinly sliced; mint leaves and herb flowers (optional)

To prepare the salmon, combine salt, sugar, lime zest and gin. Gently rub this over the surface of the salmon. Place in a shallow dish and cover with plastic wrap. Chill the salmon for at least 4 hours or overnight.

When ready to prepare the salad, peel and slice the avocados.

Sprinkle the fennel with a little extra salt, and pick the watercress leaves from any thick stalks.

Toss the fennel and watercress together in a small bowl with the oil, the juice of the lime and some salt and pepper to taste.

Remove salmon from dish and pat dry with a paper towel. Slice the salmon into paper-thin slices on the diagonal, discarding the skin.

To serve, arrange the salmon around a serving plate, evenly spaced between slices of avocado. Place the fennel and watercress salad around and decorate with the lime slices, mint leaves and any spring herb flowers from the garden.

Ceviche has become one of those dishes that is springing up on menus everywhere. I first ate ceviche in Mexico and then had delicious Spanish ceviche dishes. Then I came across ceviche on a trip to Paris and those experiences were the inspiration for this and the following recipe. If you are fortunate to have access to very fresh fish, any fish can be substituted for these two recipes. Kahawai, mullet, gurnard, kingfish and even little sprats will work too.

Gurnard ceviche with melon & seaweed

SERVES 4–6
WINE MATCH: A LIGHT CHARDONNAY
BEST IN SPRING/SUMMER/AUTUMN

500g very fresh gurnard fillets, bones removed

3 limes

1 tsp sea salt flakes

4 tbsp dried green sea-lettuce seaweed

1 tbsp wholegrain mustard

5 tbsp extra virgin olive oil

3 tbsp toasted pine nuts

1 small rock melon

2 tsp pink peppercorns

Cut the fish into bite-sized pieces and place in a bowl. Grate two of the limes and add zest and juice to the fish, with the salt. Stir well and refrigerate for an hour to allow the lime juice and salt to be absorbed.

Meanwhile, rehydrate the seaweed by placing in a bowl of cold water for about 10 minutes. It will swell up and soften. Drain and chop it roughly, keeping a few sprigs back for garnish.

To make the dressing, place the juice of the remaining lime, chopped sea-lettuce, mustard and olive oil in a bowl and stir until well combined. Add extra salt to taste.

Cut the melon in half, putting one half aside. Discard the seeds and rind and chop into small pieces. Add the chopped melon and pine nuts to the dressing. Finally add the fish with the juices it is sitting in and taste everything for seasoning. You may like to add extra salt and a pinch of caster sugar.

Let the ceviche stand at room temperature for about 15 minutes. Serve the ceviche in small bowls, and place thin ribbons of remaining melon and reserved seaweed sprigs on top.

For a ceviche, fish needs to be marinated for a short time to inject a little flavour and remove any raw fishy taste. However, marinating the fish for too long will make it tough and too firm. Freshly caught kahawai is not a bait fish. Smoke it, serve as delicious sashimi or pan-fry in butter.

Kahawai ceviche with radishes, beetroot & avocado

SERVES 4–6
WINE MATCH: CHARDONNAY
BEST IN SPRING/SUMMER/AUTUMN

500g very fresh kahawai (or kingfish) skinned and boned

1 shallot, finely chopped

5cm piece of peeled fresh ginger

2 tsp salt

2 large lemons

4 small radishes

1 small beetroot, peeled and cut into thin matchsticks

2 tbsp chopped dill

4 tbsp citrus olive oil

1 avocado, cut into cubes

Cut the fish into bite-sized pieces and place in a glass or stainless steel bowl. Add the shallot and grate the ginger in with a fine grater. Add the salt with the finely grated zest and the juice of the lemons. Toss together so it is well mixed and cover with plastic wrap. Refrigerate for at least one hour.

Meanwhile, wash the radishes and slice as thinly as possible – a mandolin is perfect for this. Place in iced water until needed.

Prepare the beetroot but keep it separated from everything else as the juices will run and turn everything bright pink.

When ready to serve, toss the radishes, dill and citrus olive oil into the marinated fish, retaining all the juices. Carefully stir together and taste for seasoning. You may need to add more lemon or more salt. Add the avocado chunks to the ceviche and finally toss in the delicate beetroot matchsticks.

Serve in bowls. You may like to accompany the ceviche with thin toast or corn chips.

For this recipe, which was inspired by several bowls of a delicious stew I ate while touring around the coast of Portugal, I have used diamond shell clams, a local taonga here in New Zealand. Sweet and meaty, they are prized by our chefs, who can order them freshly harvested from the sandy base in deep waters off Cloudy Bay, Marlborough. You should try them straight from the shell while fresh and tangy. They can be shucked with a sharp knife, but for many people a far easier way to open the clams is to pop them in the freezer. After about two hours, remove them and place on a shallow platter. As they thaw the shells will open of their own accord. Serve at once. If this process is done swiftly, nothing is lost in the process.

Portuguese-style clam stew

SERVES 4
WINE SUGGESTION: CABERNET BLEND
BEST IN ANY SEASON

1 tbsp extra virgin olive oil

6 spicy sausages

1 red onion, thinly sliced

pinch of cayenne pepper

1kg diamond shell clams, scrubbed

4 medium tomatoes, coarsely chopped

1 clove garlic

a large handful of roughly chopped coriander

1 cup dry white wine or light stock

Heat the olive oil in a wide pan. Remove the skin from the sausages, break them into small pieces and add to the pan with the onion and cook over moderate heat, stirring occasionally, until the onion softens and the sausage begins to brown. This should take about 5–10 minutes. Stir in the cayenne, add the clams and top with the tomatoes, garlic and half of the coriander. Add the wine or stock and bring to a simmer. Cover the pan and cook for a few minutes until all the clams have opened.

To finish, scatter over the remaining coriander and serve in bowls with spoons. Remember to provide an extra bowl for discarded clam shells.

We have a burgeoning farmed-oyster industry in New Zealand. It is only a few years since wild-caught Bluff oysters reigned supreme, but now connoisseurs find favour with Pacific oysters fresh from marine farms around the country and increasingly can identify an oyster's origin by the taste. Oysters stir up emotions for many food lovers. The appeal of different oysters is that each takes on the flavour characteristics of the waters in which they grow, thus they are most often named for the place they are raised in. They can be sweet, buttery, briny, metallic, creamy, savoury or have a slightly mineral taste as they are affected by seasonal variations in climate and temperature, the phytoplankton on which they feed, and the salinity, mineral content and tidal flow of the water. A freshly shucked oyster should be eaten immediately for best taste, and will also give hints of the sea water that is captured within the shell. For this recipe any oyster will work as the individual flavour will not be as pronounced when cooked.

Creamy oyster & leek soup

SERVES 4 GENEROUSLY
WINE SUGGESTION: CHARDONNAY
BEST IN AUTUMN/WINTER/SPRING

2 thin leeks

4 tbsp butter

2 tbsp flour

1 litre fish or chicken stock

300ml full cream milk

1 lemon, juice and zest

salt and freshly ground black pepper

2 dozen fresh oysters

Split the leeks down their length with a sharp knife and wash them by running under plenty of cold water. It is really important to remove all traces of soil so they are not gritty when cooked. Slice thinly into rings.

Melt the butter in a deep saucepan and add the leeks. Sauté over gentle heat until they are very tender without browning or colouring the leeks (about 15 minutes). Stir in the flour and continue to cook gently for two minutes before adding the stock. Bring to a simmer for a further 10 minutes, before adding the milk, lemon juice and zest, and continue to stir well.

Chop half the oysters into small pieces. Add these to the pan.

Use a blending stick or food processor to liquidise the soup until it is smooth and creamy. Season to taste with salt and freshly ground black pepper.

Reheat gently to serve. Garnish each serving with two or three fresh oysters and serve at once.

One of the joys of my life is working with passionate artisans and trying their products. Around New Zealand the olive oil industry is growing, with some excellent oils that range from peppery to buttery. In Martinborough, Lot 8's owner Nalini Baruch supplements the production of an excellent extra virgin olive oil with a range of fragrant infused oils. Working with chef Makoto Tokyuama at Auckland's Cocoro restaurant, she has created a world first: yuzu-infused olive oil. Yuzu, a popular Japanese citrus fruit, has a distinctive perfume. It is available online only, but any citrus-infused oil could replace it here. And often the best recipes are the most simple – simple to prepare and simple to eat.

Fresh salmon with yuzu oil & garden herbs

SERVES 4 AS AN ENTRÉE
DRINKS SUGGESTION: DRY JAPANESE SAKE
BEST IN ANY SEASON

250g fresh salmon

1 tbsp soy sauce

Sansho pepper flakes (available in Japanese grocery stores or use white pepper)

1 tbsp yuzu or citrus-flavoured olive oil

freshly picked garden herbs and baby sprouts

Using a sharp knife, slice the salmon into thin slices and lay them on a flat serving platter.

Drizzle the soy sauce over the salmon, sprinkle on some Sansho pepper flakes and then pour over the yuzu oil.

Scatter some soft-leafed garden herbs (parsley, chives, mint or baby basil), and allow to stand at room temperature for 10 minutes before serving. Pickled ginger served on the side, will add a little zing.

I'm always thinking of new ways to present fresh fish and this recipe I created became a winner as it coincided with the rising popularity of turmeric, now considered a wonder spice for its health advantages. We cook our fish like this often. Spices should never be stored too long as they lose their pungency quite quickly once they are ground. Shop often for spices and be bold about any that have been in the pantry for more than a year. Toss them out and replace them with freshly purchased spices – your food will taste far better.

Turmeric & lime fish fillets

SERVES 4
WINE SUGGESTION: A DELICATE RIESLING
BEST IN ANY SEASON

4 x 180g fillets firm fish (John Dory, flounder, orange roughy or turbot)

½ tsp salt

1 tsp ground turmeric

2 limes, juice and finely grated zest

2 tsp finely grated ginger

1 clove garlic, crushed

2 tbsp flour

4 tbsp grapeseed oil

Lay the fish fillets on a plate. Combine the salt, turmeric, lime juice and zest, ginger and garlic together in a small bowl and mix well. Rub this mixture over the fish on all sides and then cover with cling film and refrigerate for 30 minutes.

When ready to fry the fish, shake off excess moisture and dust the fillets lightly with the flour.

Heat the oil in a heavy frying pan and when hot, lay the fish in a single layer in the pan. Fry until the fish turns golden and then turn each fillet over and cook for a further minute, so the fish is just cooked through and not drying out.

Serve at once with extra lime wedges and a bowl of yogurt with chopped coriander stirred through. Excellent with potatoes or rice.

This frittata is perfect for using those pottles of already shucked oysters. Usually packed with their juices and a little fresh seawater, drain them in a sieve before using them but do not wash the oysters as the flavour will disappear down the sink.

Oyster & chive frittata

SERVES 2
WINE SUGGESTION: CHARDONNAY
BEST IN AUTUMN/WINTER/SPRING

1 dozen shucked oysters

a handful of fresh chives

6 eggs

1 tsp soy sauce

½ tsp freshly ground black pepper

2 tbsp butter

30g parmesan or sharp cheddar cheese

1 lemon

Heat the oven grill until it is hot.

Have the oysters in a small bowl and place them beside the stovetop where you will cook the eggs. Finely chop about three quarters of the chives, leaving a few perfect chives whole for garnish.

Break the eggs into a bowl and whisk with the soy sauce and black pepper.

Heat an ovenproof frying pan and add the butter. When the butter is almost browning, ladle the egg mixture into the pan, swirling it around so it coats the pan evenly. As the edges of the eggs cook, draw them toward the centre with a fork, lifting the pan a little so that uncooked egg reaches the edges and cooks. Work quickly and continue to do this until the egg is thickly rippled and almost cooked through.

Quickly strew the oysters evenly over the surface of the egg, scatter with the chopped chives and then grate the cheese over the frittata. Pop the pan under the heated grill for about 2 minutes so the oysters firm up a little.

To serve, slide the frittata on to a plate and decorate with whole chives and thin lemon wedges.

Salmon is always a welcome item on any celebratory menu. Inspired by a fleeting visit to St Petersburg, where the food was mostly underwhelming (although the caviar was sublime!), I recreated one of the few dishes I had really enjoyed there for a family Christmas feast. This is my version of the famed salmon coulibiac, a tasty pie with fresh salmon, rice, egg and spinach.

Salmon coulibiac

SERVES 8–10
WINE SUGGESTION: CHARDONNAY OR CHAMPAGNE
BEST IN ANY SEASON

1kg piece of skinned and boned fresh salmon
salt and freshly ground black pepper
500g spinach
1 cup cooked long grain rice
3 eggs, hardboiled and shelled
1 cup finely chopped garden herbs (parsley, mint, basil, chives)
500g flaky puff pastry (Paneton pre-rolled)
1 lemon, juice only
1 extra egg for glazing

Skin the salmon and season with salt and pepper. If the piece is not an even oblong shape, cut it into 2 pieces down the middle lengthwise. Set aside.

Wash the spinach and cook in a small amount of salted water until it wilts. Refresh under cold water; drain and squeeze out thoroughly. This is important as any residue water will leak out into the pie. Chop finely and place in a bowl with the rice. Also chop the egg and add to the spinach and rice with the herbs, salt and pepper. Mix well.

Roll out half the pastry into a rectangle about 6cm larger than the salmon, and place on a paper-lined baking tray. Spread half the spinach mixture along the centre so it covers about two-thirds of the pastry, leaving a strip of about 6cm on all sides. Place the salmon in the centre, topping and tailing it so the shape roughly equates to an oblong. Sprinkle over extra salt and pepper with a squeeze of lemon juice.

Spread the remaining spinach and rice mixture over the salmon. Roll and place remaining pastry on top, sealing the pastry base together by brushing the edges with the beaten egg to form a neat, closed parcel. Brush the whole parcel with beaten egg. Return to the refrigerator for at least half an hour, then bake at 200°C for about 20 minutes until pastry is crisp and golden and the salmon is cooked. Allow the coulibiac to rest for at least 10 minutes before cutting into slices.

I love clams. I love fresh corn. I love summer. All those things come together here for a real summery dish. Once the corn is over, you could always omit it and just feast on clams with this excellent dressing. It is perfect with any fresh clams from the New Zealand coast including pipi, tuatua, storm clams or other shellfish like greenlip mussels.

Clams with corn & chilli

SERVES 6 OR 8 AS A PRE-DINNER SNACK
WINE SUGGESTION: SAUVIGNON BLANC
BEST IN SUMMER

Herb dressing:

1 cup parsley and dill

6 tbsp citrus olive oil

salt and pepper

Chilli sauce:

1 red pepper

2 red chillies

3 ripe tomatoes, skinned and seeds removed

salt to taste

Clams:

1kg diamond shell clams

1 cup sauvignon blanc

2 corn cobs, cut into chunks

Make the herb dressing, chop the parsley and dill and place in a liquidiser with the oil and mix to a paste. Season with salt and pepper to taste.

For the chilli sauce, roast the pepper and chillies until blistered and soft. Discard skin and seeds and place in a liquidiser with the tomatoes. Mix until smooth and season with salt and pepper to taste.

Steam the diamond shell clams open in a large pan with a cup of sauvignon blanc.

Cook the corn by steaming or grilling. Season to taste.

Remove one half of each shell and sit the clams on a platter with the corn pieces. Spoon a little of the sauces over the clams and serve while warm or at room temperature.

Cucumber is mostly thought of as a salad ingredient, but cucumbers also make a great cooked vegetable – perfect to add to stir-fries and curries. I like to peel and then cut the cucumber right through the middle lengthwise, removing most of the seeds. If the dish is cooked for longer than a few minutes towards the end of preparation, the seeds tend to separate and float around in the curry.

Salmon & cucumber green curry

SERVES 4–6
WINE SUGGESTION: CHARDONNAY
BEST IN SUMMER/AUTUMN

6 medium red potatoes (red rascal)

1 medium fennel bulb

2 medium cucumbers

3 cups baby spinach leaves

500g fresh salmon

2 tbsp vegetable oil

1 packet green curry paste

1 cup vegetable stock

300ml coconut cream

2 limes

salt to taste

handful of fresh coriander leaves

Wash the potatoes and cut into 4cm pieces. Slice the fennel. Peel the cucumbers, remove the seeds and cut into small chunks. Wash the spinach well and cut the salmon into 5cm cubes.

Heat the oil in a large pan and add the potatoes and fennel. Toss well over the heat and add the curry paste. Stir this in well and cook so the curry paste becomes fragrant and coats the potatoes and fennel. Add the vegetable stock and bring to a simmer. Cover and cook until the potatoes are cooked.

Add the cucumber and simmer for a minute or two longer.

(The curry can be prepared to this point and refrigerated until you wish to finish the dish and serve.)

Stir in the coconut cream and return the curry to a simmer. Add the salmon and spinach leaves and allow this to simmer for no more than two minutes, so the salmon cooks through and the spinach wilts.

Taste for seasoning and add salt if necessary with the juice of one of the limes.

To serve, ladle into bowls and garnish with coriander leaves and lime wedges. Serve with steamed rice.

I do wish that travellers journeying around our country were able to more easily access the specialties of each region. Not all restaurants and cafés are conscientiously dedicated to promoting the local food, but when they do it can be a magical experience – especially if matched with local wines. Marlborough, world famous for its wine, is also a strong food-producing region, and this chowder was inspired by the wonderful salmon and mussels that are raised in the beautiful Marlborough Sounds. Perfect food when accompanied by a local sauvignon blanc.

Mussel & salmon chowder

SERVES 6
WINE SUGGESTION: MARLBOROUGH SAUVIGNON BLANC
BEST IN ANY SEASON

18 fresh mussels

200ml white wine

2 tbsp butter

2 bulbs fennel, finely sliced

2 cloves garlic, finely chopped

2 medium potatoes, peeled and diced

1 small pinch saffron threads

pinch of sweet paprika

1 tbsp flour

800ml fish stock

150ml cream

200g fresh salmon, cut into cubes

fresh parsley for garnish

Place the mussels in a saucepan with the wine, cover with the lid and bring to a gentle simmer until the mussels all pop open. Take most of the mussels from the shells, remove the beard and the foot from each and place them in a small bowl covered with a little of the liquid that has been released from the shellfish. This will keep the mussels moist and tender. Leave six mussels in the shell for garnish when serving.

Melt the butter in a deep saucepan and add the fennel and garlic, tossing well over the heat until the fennel starts to soften. Add the potatoes with the saffron and paprika and stir well over the heat for a further 4–5 minutes. Stir in the flour, add the fish stock and stir with a wooden spoon until the liquid comes to a simmer. Allow to simmer very gently for 10 minutes.

To finish, add the cream, salmon and the mussels with the mussel liquid. Return the pan to a simmer and cook just long enough for the mussels to reheat and the salmon to cook, adding in the six reserved mussels.

Garnish with chopped parsley and serve piping hot with crusty bread and lemon wedges on the side.

SECTION 4
Meat matters

124 Lamb salad with radish, watercress & watermelon
126 Herbed lamb in a vegetable ragout
128 Leg of lamb with minty feta sauce
130 Rajasthan lamb curry
132 Lamb shanks with orange, tomato & olives
134 *Food talk: The great NZ roast dinner*
136 Beef meatballs in spicy tomato sauce
138 Star anise marinated beef
140 Fried tofu with spicy minced pork
142 Pork shoulder with apple & parsley stuffing
144 Cabbage & pork rolls in savoury broth
146 Braised red cabbage with spicy pork chops
148 Pork braised in milk
150 Venison winter salad
152 Venison salad with pine nuts, feta & beetroot
154 Venison sliders
156 Roast venison with spinach, dates & orange

Make this pretty salad on a hot summer's evening when you're seeking a refreshing light meal but still want to impress. Small lamb fillets or tenderloins are delicious. Take care cooking them as they can become a little tough if cooked too long.

Lamb salad with radish, watercress & watermelon

SERVES 4
WINE SUGGESTION: A CHILLED CRISP RIESLING
BEST IN SUMMER

300g lamb fillets or tenderloins

2 tbsp sesame oil

2 lemons

salt and freshly ground black pepper

6 small firm radishes

2 cups baby watercress leaves

2 thick slices watermelon (250g)

½ cup small basil leaves and flowers

Dressing:

1 lemon, zest and juice

3 tbsp grapeseed oil

salt and freshly ground black pepper

Trim the fat and sinew from the lamb.

In a bowl combine the sesame oil, finely grated zest and the juice of the lemons with a little salt and freshly ground black pepper. Mix this all together, add the lamb and let it marinate for up to an hour.

Meanwhile prepare the other ingredients. Wash the radishes and cut them into paper-thin slices with a sharp knife or a Japanese mandolin.

Wash the watercress, drying it in a clean tea towel or a salad spinner. Cut any tough stalks off and discard them.

Remove the watermelon rind and cut the flesh into nice even chunks.

Make the dressing by shaking the lemon zest and juice, grapeseed oil and some salt and pepper together.

Heat a barbecue grill or a ridged grill pan until hot. Cook the lamb over medium heat until golden brown on both sides, but still a little springy to the touch. Allow the lamb to rest while you make the salad.

Toss the radishes, watercress, watermelon and the basil together, adding most of the dressing. Spread this on a serving platter or divide between four dinner plates.

Slice the lamb thinly and place on top of the salad, garnishing with the basil flowers. Tip the remaining dressing over the lamb and serve at once.

We are all mindful of eating smaller portions of food for our health, particularly red meat. However some of those special cuts of meat that seem almost out of reach due to cost can go quite a long way if served judiciously. Lamb back straps and fillets are totally delicious and when served with plenty of vegetables we really do not need large servings. This is a delightful way to serve young, tender lamb with young, tender vegetables.

Herbed lamb in a vegetable ragout

SERVES 4
WINE SUGGESTION: ROSÉ
BEST IN SPRING/SUMMER

2 tbsp olive oil

2 tbsp seeded mustard

½ cup fresh rosemary

salt and pepper

2 back straps of lamb

Ragout and broth:

2 cups well-flavoured chicken stock

pinch of saffron powder

12 baby carrots, trimmed and cleaned

8 thin spring onions

1 cup broad beans, shelled and blanched

1 cup snowpeas, trimmed

1 cup tender young green beans

3 tbsp finely chopped mint and parsley

Mix the olive oil, mustard and rosemary and season with salt and freshly ground black pepper. Coat the lamb with this and leave to absorb the flavours while you deal with the vegetables.

Bring the stock to a simmer and add the saffron. Place the carrots and spring onions in the broth and gently cook for about ten minutes until they soften.

Meanwhile squeeze the blanched broad beans from their shells and combine with the snowpeas and beans, ready to add to the vegetable ragout.

Heat a ridged grill pan or heavy frying pan and when hot, add the lamb back straps. Sear on all sides then reduce the heat and cook gently for about 3–4 minutes each side. Remove and cover with foil to rest the lamb.

Add the broad beans, snowpeas and beans to the broth and simmer for 2–3 minutes. Taste the broth and adjust seasoning if necessary.

To serve, ladle a little of the broth into four shallow plates. Distribute the vegetables evenly between the four plates. Slice the lamb into diagonal pieces and lay 3 slices on each plate.

Finish by scattering over the mint and parsley with a little extra freshly ground pepper.

We wouldn't be Kiwis without our love of feasting on a whole leg of lamb for a special get-together dinner. This recipe ensures the lamb is really tasty as it is first marinated in a blend that combines spice, herb, lemon, anchovy and garlic. Once the lamb is cooked and ready to serve, there's a special zesty sauce to enhance the flavours and to make it look truly festive. This was originally cooked for a family Christmas dinner feature in the *Listener* but would grace any special occasion.

Leg of lamb with minty feta sauce

SERVES 10–12
WINE SUGGESTION: A RICH PINOT NOIR
BEST IN ALL SEASONS

1 leg spring lamb

For the marinade:

2 tsp ground cumin

2 tbsp preserved lemon, finely chopped

6 anchovies, finely chopped

2 tbsp rosemary, finely chopped

1 clove garlic

1 tbsp olive oil

For the sauce:

250g soft feta cheese

250ml Greek yogurt

2 tbsp lemon juice

1 tsp salt

1 tsp freshly ground black pepper

4 tbsp mint, tarragon, basil or dill leaves, chopped

extra herb leaves for garnish

1 pomegranate, seeds only (or dried cranberries)

Pound the marinade ingredients together in a pestle and mortar or whizz up until almost finely chopped in the food processor. Cut 2cm slashes in the lamb and rub the marinade into the cuts and over the surface. Cover and leave overnight in the refrigerator for the flavours to be absorbed into the meat.

To make the sauce, combine all the listed ingredients, except the extra herb leaves and pomegranate seeds, in a food processor or blender until smooth. Refrigerate until needed.

To cook the lamb, preheat the oven or charcoal barbecue to 190°C. Place the lamb in a small roasting pan if cooking in the oven and place this in the middle of the oven. If using the barbecue make sure the coals are glowing and place the lamb directly on the grill. Roast the meat for about one hour and ten minutes, then pierce with a skewer to ensure the juices are almost clear.

When cooked but still juicy, remove from the heat, cover with foil and allow the meat to rest for about 15 minutes.

Carve into neat slices and spoon over the sauce, topped with the extra leaves and pomegranate seeds. Fresh cherries as a garnish will give a more festive look.

Early season lamb is tender, delicious and sweet. It must be carefully cooked so that the meat has at the very least a pink tinge, is juicy, and is rested and covered for about ten minutes before serving. Pan-frying, grilling, cooking over coals on a barbecue or gentle roasting are all recommended for early-season lamb. Later in the season when lamb meat is more robust in flavour, braise or slow roast lamb for longer periods until the meat is thoroughly cooked but still moist with pan juices or stock, as in this delicious curry.

Rajasthan lamb curry

SERVES 4
DRINKS SUGGESTION: ICY LAGER BEER
BEST IN WINTER

1kg lamb shoulder chops

½ tsp salt

2 fresh red chillies, finely chopped

2 tbsp sweet paprika

4 tbsp vegetable oil or ghee

2 cinnamon sticks, broken into 2–3 pieces

1 tsp cloves

10 cardamom pods

1 red onion, finely chopped

5cm piece of ginger, peeled and finely grated

3 cloves garlic, peeled and crushed

1 tsp ground coriander seeds

2 cups water

3 tbsp chopped fresh coriander

Cut the lamb into 3–4cm chunks. Mix the salt, chillies and paprika together and toss the lamb in this mixture so it is completely coated. Leave aside for about 30 minutes for the flavours to be absorbed.

Heat the oil or ghee in a large, heavy casserole dish. When hot, add the cinnamon, cloves and cardamom. Let these spices sizzle for a few seconds, then add the red onion. Reduce the heat and stir the onion and spices until the onion turns golden brown. Add the ginger, garlic and ground coriander and stir over the heat for a further minute.

Turn up the heat and add the lamb immediately, stirring constantly so that it browns a little. Pour in the water and bring to the boil. Cover the dish with a heavy lid and simmer gently on the stove top for about 70–80 minutes or until the dish is very tender. Check often to ensure the lamb does not dry out, adding extra water if necessary, but the final result should be very thick with the sauce clinging to the meat. If the sauce is too thin, simmer rapidly for a minute or two to reduce it.

To serve, sprinkle over the fresh coriander leaves and accompany with naan or any other Indian flatbread.

When the first of the juicy New Zealand oranges are in fruit-and-vegetable stores I cannot get enough of them. They're packed with lovely flavours and goodness, and I am always inspired to use them to make a real treat: slowly braised lamb shanks. In this recipe I add a dollop of a rather special product, Simo's Orange & Cinnamon Zest, produced and bottled by Chef Simo who has an authentic Moroccan delicatessen and eatery in Christchurch. His products are available online but if you cannot find this one, add lots of extra grated orange zest.

Lamb shanks with orange, tomato & olives

SERVES 4
WINE SUGGESTION: SYRAH
BEST IN WINTER

4 lamb shanks

2 tbsp finely chopped thyme

2 tbsp olive oil

1 large onion

1 tbsp Simo's Orange and Cinnamon Zest

1 cup syrah

1 can crushed tomatoes in juice

1 orange, juice and zest cut into fine julienne strips

salt and pepper

3 tbsp pitted olives

pappardelle noodles

3 tbsp chopped Italian parsley

Preheat the oven to 180°C.

Scatter the lamb shanks with thyme. Heat the oil in a heavy frying pan and brown the lamb on all sides. (This will help to get rid of some of the extra fat.)

Finely slice the onion. Remove the shanks from the pan and place in a casserole dish.

Tip some of the extra fat away from the frying pan and add the onion to the remaining fat. Cook the onion gently and as it softens, add the Orange and Cinnamon Zest, (or extra grated zest if needed). When the onion is nicely browned and crisp, add the wine to the pan. Allow this to bubble up for a minute or two then add the tomatoes with their juice and the julienned zest and juice of the orange. Bring this all to a simmer, and add a little salt and pepper to taste.

Pour this liquid over the lamb shanks in the casserole dish, cover tightly with the lid and place in the heated oven. After 1 hour, add the olives and continue to cook for another 30 minutes. Check once or twice to ensure the liquid is not drying up, adding a little water if necessary.

While the lamb is cooking, drop the pasta ribbons into boiling salted water and cook according to the packet instructions. Drain, toss in a little extra olive oil and use immediately.

To serve, divide the pasta between 4 plates and top with a lamb shank, extra sauce and freshly chopped parsley.

Food Talk //
The great New Zealand roast dinner

Many of us grew up in households where a roast meal with all the trimmings graced our dinner table at least once a week. There's no denying New Zealand is a lucky country, with an economy founded on the income our farmers and their produce earned locally, and internationally in export markets. As we've assimilated other cultures into our own, travelled to experience diverse flavours, and connected the dots between health and diet, the emphasis on meat has changed. But the majority of Kiwis still love meat. Anyone who cooks a roast for friends is bound to score praise, although the roast now is more a special-occasion feast than the twice-weekly family meal.

Whether the choice is beef, lamb, pork, venison or chicken, there are certain expectations of what should be alongside the meat. Guests will cry out for a savoury gravy, crisp roast potatoes and some fresh green vegetables. There are several excellent roast meat recipes in this book, including a stunning lamb leg and my ultimate roast chicken. I am also including here a roast beef, with vital information on how to make gravy, essential roast potatoes and traditional Yorkshire puddings. Many cuts of beef can be roasted but a great piece of sirloin, with a healthy coating of fat, is my favourite. The secret to juicy meat that's rare and succulent is to ensure the beef stands for at least 20 minutes once it leaves the oven, well covered and warm before carving.

HOW TO MAKE A GOOD GRAVY
The tastiest gravy does not require flavour booster, marmite or a pouch of gravy mix. What you need is some well-flavoured stock appropriate to the roast it will accompany. If you haven't any good stock, a cup or so of wine will be fine. You also need a spoonful of flour and the drippings and residue the meat has left in the pan during the roasting process. Place the pan the meat was cooked in over gentle heat and tip the flour in. Stir vigorously with a wooden spoon to scrape up any residue that sticks to the bottom. Allow the flour to brown slightly in the fat. If there is a lot of fat, tip some into a small container and reserve for another use. Add the stock, wine (or water if you must) and continually stir until the gravy comes to the boil. Turn the heat down very low and allow the gravy to bubble gently until ready to serve. If you turn your back and the gravy seems to have disappeared with all the moisture evaporating, do not add more stock as it will intensify in flavour and saltiness. Simply add a little more water, and always taste the gravy for seasoning and adjust to taste.

BEST-EVER ROAST POTATOES
Roast potatoes must be crunchy on the outside but fluffy and tender within. Agrias are the best potato for roasting. Par-boil them, then drain them really well. Meanwhile place 2 tablespoons of oil and butter in a roasting pan in the oven. Rough up the surface of the potatoes and toss them in the oil and butter mixture. Sprinkle with salt and pepper and roast for about 50 minutes shaking the pan occasionally.

Roast sirloin of beef with horseradish gravy

WINE SUGGESTION: PINOT NOIR

- 1.5–2kg beef sirloin in the piece
- 2 tbsp extra virgin olive oil
- 3 tbsp horseradish mustard
- 2 tbsp finely chopped fresh thyme
- 1 tbsp salt
- freshly ground black pepper
- 2 tbsp flour
- 500ml beef stock

Pre-heat the oven to 220°C. Pat the beef dry, and tie tightly at regular 5cm intervals so it will hold its shape. Mix the olive oil, 2 tablespoons of the mustard, thyme, salt and a little pepper in a bowl. Spread over the surface of the meat on the underside, keeping some to spread over the layer of fat on top. Place the beef in a roasting pan in the oven. Turn the oven down to 200°C after 10 minutes and continue to roast the beef for a further 20–30 minutes, depending how rare you like your meat.

Take from the oven, and let the beef rest for at least 20 minutes, well covered with foil and a large towel.

Follow the instructions on the previous page to make a delicious gravy, adding the horseradish mustard just before the stock and continually stirring until the gravy comes to the boil, then simmer.

Carve the meat into slices, place on a heated platter and pour a little gravy over, handing the rest separately in a jug.

Herbed Yorkshire puddings

- 120g flour
- 1 egg and 1 yolk
- salt and pepper
- 200ml full cream milk
- 4 tbsp thyme and parsley, finely chopped
- 4 tbsp olive oil

Mix the flour, egg and yolk, salt and pepper and milk together by beating until smooth.

Stir in the herbs and allow this batter to stand for at least one hour.

Heat the muffin pan in a 200°C oven with a little smear of oil in each of the pans. Pour the batter in and cook in the oven until puffed and golden, about 20 minutes.

Serve with the roasted beef and gravy. Makes about 18 mini Yorkshire puddings.

Who doesn't love a meatball? Juicy, meaty and perfect food for both young and old. I like to use sourdough breadcrumbs in the meatballs as the bread seems to soften the meat, making them really tender. You could also use pork, chicken or lamb mince in this recipe if you would like an even lighter meatball. And if you want your meatball sauce spicier, simply add more red pepper flakes or a large pinch of chilli powder.

Beef meatballs in spicy tomato sauce

SERVES 4
WINE SUGGESTION: CABERNET BLEND
BEST IN ANY SEASON

600g minced beef

2–3 slices white sourdough bread

1 small onion, chopped

4 tbsp extra virgin olive oil

2 tbsp chopped parsley

2 tbsp chopped thyme

1 tsp paprika

salt and pepper

1 egg

Sauce:

2 tbsp extra virgin olive oil

1 onion, finely chopped

pinch of red pepper flakes

2 king sweetie peppers (or 1 large red pepper)

400g can crushed tomatoes

1 cup chicken or beef stock

salt to taste

300g spinach leaves, washed and chopped

To make the meatballs, place the beef mince in a bowl. Process the sourdough in the food processor to become breadcrumbs and add this to the mince.

Toss the chopped onion in one tablespoon of the oil in a small bowl and microwave it for two minutes so it is softened and partially cooked. Allow to cool a little before adding to the mince with the parsley, thyme, paprika, salt and pepper and the egg. Mix this well with your hands and form little meatballs, each about the size of a golf ball.

Heat the remaining 3 tablespoons of oil in a heavy frying pan and brown the meatballs on all sides. You may need to do this in a couple of batches so they brown rather than stew. Keep the meatballs aside.

To make the sauce, heat the oil in a heavy pan, and add the onion. Cook over a gentle heat until it is golden. Add the red pepper flakes and cook for another minute.

Chop the peppers into very small strips and add to the onion, continuing to stir and cook until they are soft. Add the tomato and stock and bring to a simmer. Allow the sauce to simmer for 20 to 30 minutes until thick and unctuous. Taste and season well.

To finish, add the meatballs to the sauce and allow them to simmer for 5 minutes. Add the spinach, stir in well and cook a further 2 to 3 minutes so that it wilts but is still a bright green colour.

Serve at once with rice, noodles or mashed potato.

There's endless talk about sustainability in food circles. We recognise that the economy of many households inevitably means food purchases have to be made on price alone, but where people have choices they will seek and find food that has been raised or grown with regard to the continued fertility of the land, and in the case of animals, in a manner that's kind and healthy. So like others around the planet who care, I subscribe to the belief that if you're going to eat an animal you should consider eating every part of it, not just the most choice cuts. This recipe uses the lesser-known cuts, flank steak or skirt steak, which is totally delicious.

Star anise marinated beef

SERVES 6
WINE SUGGESTION: ROSÉ
BEST IN ANY SEASON

1kg flank or skirt steak (trimmed of fat and sinew)

2 tbsp olive oil

2 cups water

½ cup soy sauce

½ cup Shaoxing wine (Chinese rice wine)

2 tbsp sugar

2 whole star anise

1 cinnamon stick

strip of orange rind

2 slices fresh ginger

1 small onion, sliced

2 spring onions

grated orange rind

Cut the meat into two strips lengthwise. Heat the oil to very hot in a frying pan and brown the strips on all sides. Drain on a paper towel.

Put all the remaining ingredients in a deep wide saucepan and bring to a simmer. Add the browned beef strips and simmer slowly over a low heat for 90 minutes or until the beef is very tender. Leave to cool in the liquid. Refrigerate until needed.

To serve, take the cold meat from the broth and slice across the grain into neat slices. Arrange the meat on a serving platter alongside a salad of seasonal greens (fennel, beans and sugar snaps), and pour salad dressing over the meat to keep it moist. Garnish with chopped spring onion and grated orange rind.

Tofu, an ingredient beloved by many vegetarians as a meat substitute, is gaining in popularity. It is made by a process that involves soaking and puréeing dried soybeans, simmering them in spring water and then adding a tiny amount of nigari (magnesium chloride) to set the tofu as it is pressed. Look for soft fresh tofu rather than the tougher, tightly packaged long-life version.

Fried tofu with spicy minced pork

SERVES 4
WINE SUGGESTION: CABERNET BLEND
BEST IN ANY SEASON

600g fresh firm tofu

2 tbsp flour

1 small onion, finely chopped

2 tbsp rice bran oil

1 tbsp grated ginger

1 clove garlic, crushed

400g pork mince

400g can crushed tomatoes in juice

dash of Tabasco sauce

1 tbsp soy sauce

2 tbsp mirin (rice wine)

freshly ground black pepper

2 tbsp chopped parsley

¼ cup rice bran oil

Cut the tofu into 5cm cubes, dust very lightly with flour and keep aside until ready to fry.

To make the sauce, cook the onion in a heated pan with oil over gentle heat until softened and starting to brown. Add the ginger, garlic and mince, turn up the heat and cook for 5–6 minutes, watching carefully until it browns.

Add the tomatoes with the Tabasco, soy sauce, mirin and black pepper and simmer over a very gentle heat for 30 minutes, stirring occasionally and adding water if it dries out.

Add the parsley and taste for seasoning.

In a separate pan, heat the oil and when hot, sauté the tofu so it browns nicely on all sides.

To serve, drain the tofu on paper towels, place on a serving platter and spoon over some of the spicy mince mixture.

Serve at once with a green salad on the side.

My favourite cut of pork is the shoulder as it has plenty of fat to keep the meat moist and juicy. Pork can be rich, however, so I always think it needs to be balanced with a hit of salt, sweetness and acidity. The bacon adds the saltiness, the apple adds sweetness and the orange juice gives a little hint of acidity to the delicious stuffing.

Pork shoulder with apple & parsley stuffing

SERVES 6
WINE SUGGESTION: SYRAH
BEST IN AUTUMN/WINTER

1kg boned shoulder of NZ pork, skin separated and scored

4 tbsp vegetable oil

1 onion, finely chopped

2 rashers bacon, cut into thin matchsticks

1 apple, peeled and finely diced

½ cup wholemeal breadcrumbs

1 orange, juice and grated zest

½ cup chopped parsley

750g peeled kumara

Preheat the oven to 200°C. Make a stuffing by heating the oil, and cooking the onion and bacon until soft and fragrant. Remove from the heat and add apple, breadcrumbs, orange and parsley. Mix well together and season to taste. Lay the pork out with the fat side on the bench and stretch it out, making small cuts so it becomes an oblong shape. Spread the stuffing over the inner surface and tie the meat at 3cm intervals into a roll. Season with salt and pepper and a little extra parsley.

Meanwhile boil kumara, then simmer for 10 minutes. Strain the kumara, retaining the cooking liquid for the gravy.

Place the pork in a roasting pan and lay the skin over the top. This will become the crackling. Place the par-boiled kumara around the pork and add the remaining oil. Roast for 60 minutes, turning oven down to 180°C after 20 minutes. Test the pork is cooked by piercing with a skewer and the juices should run clear. If the crackling has not bubbled up and blistered, place it under the grill but watch carefully as it will burn easily.

Remove the meat and kumara to a hot platter. Add 2 tablespoons of flour to the pan and stir with the pan juices. Add kumara water, a splash of white wine and allow to bubble and thicken.

Slice the pork, break the crackling into strips and serve with the kumara and gravy.

These cabbage rolls are really tasty and so easy to prepare as the mince mixture does not need to be cooked ahead. It can be prepared, rolled in the cabbage leaves and refrigerated before poaching in the stock. It's worth having a strong-flavoured stock or broth for this soup as it is an important component of the dish.

Cabbage & pork rolls in savoury broth

SERVES 6
WINE SUGGESTION: PINOT NOIR
BEST IN AUTUMN/WINTER

For the cabbage and pork rolls:

1 head of cabbage

500g pork mince

2 rashers streaky bacon, finely chopped

1 clove garlic, crushed

100g shiitake mushrooms, finely chopped

½ teaspoon black pepper

10 sage leaves, chopped

1 slice stale white bread, crusts removed and crumbled

1 egg, lightly beaten

1 teaspoon salt

For the broth:

2 litres well-flavoured beef or chicken stock

2 tomatoes, peeled, de-seeded and diced

extra sage leaves

a little butter

parsley, chopped

Carefully separate the leaves of the cabbage, making sure you have 12 perfect leaves. Bring a large pot of salted water to the boil and simmer the leaves gently for 5 minutes. Drain well.

Mix the pork, bacon, garlic, chopped mushrooms, pepper, chopped herbs and bread crumbs together. Add the beaten egg and salt and work the mixture into a paste with your hands.

Divide the mixture into 12 pieces and shape these into cylindrical shapes. Then roll a cabbage leaf around each piece of pork, tucking the ends in and secure with a couple of toothpicks.

Bring the stock to a gentle simmer in a large wide pan.

Add the cabbage parcels and poach them for at least 15 minutes in barely simmering water. Turn them over halfway through the cooking process.

Place two parcels on each plate, removing the toothpicks.

Add the diced tomato and parsley to the broth, reheat and ladle soup over the cabbage rolls. For garnish, fry sage leaves in a little butter to make them crisp. Accompany with warm ciabatta bread.

Red cabbage is synonymous with winter. A rather hearty vegetable, it always adds brilliant colour to any plate, and is the epitome of wintry foods to match dark gamey meats, spicy pork or duck. This method of cooking cabbage was inspired by a dish I had a few years back at The Engine Room on Auckland's North Shore and is particularly good with a pork chop that has that vital coating of a little tasty fat.

Braised red cabbage with spicy pork chops

SERVES 4
WINE SUGGESTION: CABERNET BLEND
BEST IN LATE AUTUMN/WINTER

½ red cabbage

1 red-skinned apple

1 red onion

2 tbsp butter

2 tbsp olive oil

4 tbsp red wine vinegar

½ cup red wine

salt and pepper

For the pork chop:

4 meaty pork chops

1 tbsp five spice mixture

salt to taste

2 tbsp olive oil

1 tbsp butter

Slice the cabbage finely. Core the apple and cut into thin slices. Finely slice the onion.

Melt the butter and oil together in a deep pan, and add the onion and apple. Cook over gentle heat until they soften and start to turn golden (about 10 minutes).

Add the cabbage and toss everything together over the heat until it is mixed. Add the vinegar and red wine, stirring in well and allow the liquid to come to a gentle simmer.

Cook for about 25 minutes, stirring often until the cabbage is soft and glossy and the liquid has been absorbed. Check for taste, adding salt and pepper as necessary.

Meanwhile prepare the pork chops. Pat them dry and rub the five spice mixture into the meat.

Heat a heavy frying pan and add the oil and butter. Place the chops in the pan and cook over a gentle heat, turning occasionally until crisp and cooked through.

To serve, pile the cabbage onto 4 heated plates and top each with a pork chop. There will be cabbage left over and this can be reheated for another meal. It is especially good fried in a little extra butter or added to a stir-fry at the last minute.

This is hardly a rush-into-the-kitchen-and-throw-something-on-for-dinner dish, as the pork and milk is a combination that is delightful but needs long slow cooking. The milk curdles but those curds that form are almost the most delicious part of the dish and the pork will fall apart and, as they say, could be eaten with a spoon.

Pork braised in milk

SERVES 4–6
WINE SUGGESTION: CHARDONNAY
BEST IN AUTUMN/WINTER/SPRING

1.5kg free-range loin of pork, skin removed

sea salt and freshly ground black pepper

3 tbsp extra virgin olive oil

2 thin strips lemon peel

1 tsp coriander seeds

4 sage leaves

1 litre full cream milk

Remove the rind from the pork and cut away most of the fat. Season generously with salt and pepper.

Heat the olive oil in a heavy casserole dish that will fit the pork snugly. Brown the pork on all sides until it is golden and then remove to a plate so you can pour off the oil and fat.

Add the lemon peel, slightly crushed coriander seeds and sage to the dish. Return the pork to sit on top of these and pour in enough milk to come about halfway up the pork. Bring the milk to a slow simmer and cook for about 90 minutes, with the lid slightly ajar. Watch frequently and stir any skin that forms on the sides of the dish back into the liquid. Do not allow the milk to boil over, and top the milk up if it reduces too much. A golden skin will form after about one hour and the milk will curdle. This is ideal as the curds make the most delicious sauce.

When the meat is cooked and tender, remove it very carefully and carve into thin slices. Scrape up the curds and spoon them over the top.

Can be served hot or cold. Nice accompanied with a salad of fresh mixed green leaves.

Venison, whether wild or farmed, is a versatile meat that is lean and healthy. New Zealand has a sizeable venison industry and most supermarkets now stock a range of cuts that are easy to prepare. As there is never much fat on this tasty meat, small cuts should be cooked at high heat, very quickly, and hopefully served rare. If the meat is overcooked it can become rather liverish in taste. If the venison is destined for a stew or casserole it can cook much longer but it is important that it is immersed in liquid and never allowed to dry out and become chewy.

Venison winter salad

SERVES 4
WINE SUGGESTION: PINOT NOIR
BEST IN WINTER

300g venison loin in one piece

2 tbsp ground juniper berries

½ cup pomegranate juice

salt and pepper

300g pumpkin, peeled and cut into 2.5cm dice

4 tbsp vegetable oil

½ cup fresh shelled walnuts

1 small head of radicchio

1 cup baby gem lettuce leaves

2 persimmon

salt and freshly ground pepper

3 tbsp Italian parsley leaves

Marinate the venison in the juniper and pomegranate juice. Keep aside until ready to cook.

Preheat the oven to 170°C. Toss the pumpkin in 2 tablespoons of the vegetable oil and season with salt and pepper in an ovenproof dish. Place the walnuts in another small ovenproof dish. Place both dishes in the oven. Watch the walnuts carefully and as soon as they start to show any sign of colouring (about 10 minutes) remove them and allow to cool. Roast the pumpkin for 15 to 20 minutes until the pumpkin is soft and the edges are beginning to turn golden brown.

Wash the lettuce and radicchio leaves and shake them dry. Prepare the persimmon by peeling and cutting into thin slices.

Heat another 2 tablespoons of oil in a heavy frying pan, remove the venison from the marinade and season with salt and pepper. When the pan is very hot, add the venison in the whole piece and brown well on all sides. Turn down the heat and allow to cook for a further 2–3 minutes, then remove from the pan and allow the meat to rest. Tip the marinade into the pan and bring to a simmer.

To assemble the salad, toss the lettuce, radicchio, pumpkin, persimmon and walnuts together. Slice the venison and add to the salad with parsley leaves. Tip the pan juices over and serve at once.

Lots of lovely flavours meld together in this salad. Try to find a fresh goat's curd or maybe use the delicious, fresh buffalo milk cheese from Clevedon Buffalo Cheese Company. When using spinach be sure to wash it really well. Some of the bagged spinach has been grown hydroponically but if it's from an outdoor garden it is a plant that attracts dirt. I suggest soaking the spinach in a sink of cold water for at least 20 minutes.

Venison salad with pine nuts, feta & beetroot

SERVES 4
WINE SUGGESTION: PINOT NOIR
BEST IN SPRING/SUMMER/AUTUMN

500g venison (Denver leg or fillet)

For the marinade:

a few sprigs thyme, chopped

salt and freshly ground black pepper

2 tbsp olive oil

For the salad:

2 cups baby spinach leaves, washed

1 medium beetroot (cut into julienne matchsticks)

150g fresh goat cheese
(or crumbly feta)

4 tbsp pine nuts, lightly roasted

½ cup parsley and mint leaves

For the dressing:

2 tbsp balsamic vinegar

4 tbsp extra virgin olive oil

½ tsp salt

freshly ground black pepper

Place the venison in a small dish. Mix the marinade in a small bowl by chopping the thyme and adding it to the oil, salt and pepper. Pour this over the venison and allow to marinate for one hour or more.

To cook the venison, have it at room temperature and heat a frying pan until hot. Drop the venison into the pan and sear it well on all sides. If you want it a little more cooked than rare, leave it in the pan for 2–3 minutes longer, but be careful not to overcook it. Cover with foil and allow the meat to rest while you prepare the salad.

Scatter the spinach leaves evenly over a large flat salad platter. Neatly distribute the beetroot and fresh goat cheese or feta on top of the leaves.

Slice the venison and tuck the slices amongst the leaves and beetroot. Finally shake the dressing ingredients together and drizzle over everything, adding the parsley, mint leaves and pine nuts.

I am not sure when burgers became 'sliders'. There really is not a lot of difference – maybe sliders are just a tad smaller than burgers, or maybe it's just a reinvention of a name to find appeal with those who associate burgers with fast food. Either way this recipe for venison sliders is a winner, using venison mince. And there are lots of lovely vegetables to help you get your necessary 5+ a Day.

Venison sliders

MAKES 6 SLIDERS
WINE SUGGESTION: PINOT NOIR
BEST IN ANY SEASON

400g venison mince

1 small beetroot (approx. 80g)

1 medium carrot (approx. 80g)

2 tbsp finely chopped parsley

2 tsp caraway seeds

salt and freshly ground black pepper

6 small soft white buns

1 small head cos lettuce

1 avocado

100g sprouts (bean, radish, or any other fresh sprouts)

spicy fruit chutney

3 tbsp vegetable oil for frying the patties

For the dressing:

2 tbsp Dijon mustard

1 lemon, juice and zest

2 tbsp avocado oil

1 tsp salt

To make the patties, place the venison mince in a bowl. Grate the beetroot and carrot finely, using a fine microplane grater or the finest setting of your grater. Add the grated vegetables to the mince with the chopped parsley, caraway seeds and a generous seasoning of salt and pepper.

Using your hands, mix the mince really well, so that it all sticks together. Divide the mixture into six portions and with wet hands, roll into 6 balls. Place these on baking paper on a plate, pressing down a little so they are patty-shaped. Put aside or refrigerate until needed.

To prepare the other components, cut the buns in half and spread both sides generously with spicy chutney. Slice the lettuce leaves or tear into small pieces. Peel and slice the avocado. Wash and dry the sprouts.

Make the dressing by mixing the mustard, lemon juice and zest, avocado oil and salt together in a small screw-top jar.

Heat the vegetable oil in a heavy frying pan. When it is hot add the patties and turn down the heat. Cook the patties for about 3–4 minutes on the first side, then flip them and cook for a further 2–3 minutes. Choose how well cooked you would like the meat, but remember, venison is always better on the rare side than overcooked.

Place a patty on half a bun, top with lettuce, avocado and sprouts drizzled with the dressing, the top of the slider, and serve.

I've always loved the idea of a warm salad. This salad meal is great for hot weather when you do not want to hang out in the kitchen for long. Put together some exciting ingredients like orange segments and fresh sweet dates with chilled salad leaves and then top them with the venison that's still warm and juicy. Everything tastes fresh and interesting and the warm meat absorbs the spicy dressing beautifully.

Roast venison with spinach, dates & orange

SERVES 4
WINE SUGGESTION: ROSÉ
BEST IN AUTUMN/WINTER/SPRING

250g venison roast

2 tbsp of your favourite spice rub

300g baby spinach leaves

10 fresh dates

2 oranges

¼ cup pumpkin seeds, toasted

1 cup mint and/or coriander leaves

2 tbsp vegetable or olive oil for frying the venison

For the dressing:

1 orange, juice and zest

4 tbsp harissa-flavoured olive oil

salt and pepper

Rub the piece of venison with your favourite spice rub and leave to stand for at least one hour.

Meanwhile assemble the other ingredients. Wash and dry the spinach leaves and remove any long stalks. Remove the stones from the dates and cut each date in half. Peel the oranges with a sharp knife, taking care to remove all the white pith, and cut the flesh into neat pieces.

Pick the herb leaves over and remove stalks.

To make the spicy orange dressing, mix the juice and zest of the orange with the oil, salt and pepper.

Preheat the oven to 190°C. Heat the oil in a heavy frying pan until very hot. Sear the venison on all sides, then pop the pan in the oven. Roast for 4–6 minutes, then remove it from the pan, wrap in foil and allow the meat to rest for at least 10 minutes before slicing into slices. The venison should be very rare, but if you like it more well-cooked, roast for an extra 2–3 minutes.

To assemble the dish, pile the spinach onto a serving platter. Nestle the dates and orange pieces amongst the leaves. Scatter over the pumpkin seeds and herbs. Slice the venison thinly and add the warm slices on top. Drizzle over the dressing and serve.

SECTION 5

Winging it

160 Miso caramel chicken nibbles
162 Chicken livers with shallots & apples
164 Roast chicken salad with nectarines & summer leaves
166 Chicken & vegetable soup
168 Chicken dumplings with braised broad beans, lemon & mint
170 Chicken, leek & bacon pie
172 Casseroled chicken with fennel, potatoes, olives & preserved lemon
174 *Food talk: Which wine with that food?*
176 The ultimate roast chicken
178 Poussins with pears & parsley
180 Tray-baked chicken with potatoes & apricots
182 Baked chicken, leek & pumpkin
184 Three-bean salad with lemon & sliced duck breast
186 Duck & mandarin ragout

Sticky and delicious – it's so worth getting your fingers really messy with these chicken wings. The marinade made with miso paste for these chicken wings can also be used as a sauce. You can brush it over salmon, pork belly or beef ribs before pan-frying or roasting, to add succulence. Everyone loves this salty caramel flavour. It will keep well in a screw-top jar in the fridge.

Miso caramel chicken nibbles

SERVES 6
WINE SUGGESTION: CHARDONNAY
BEST IN ANY SEASON

200g caster sugar

100ml water

2 tbsp miso paste

1kg free-range chicken nibbles or wings

2 cups baby rocket leaves

1 cup microgreens or mesclun

cucumber ribbons

Take extreme care while making this as the caramel gets very hot and could cause a serious burn.

Dissolve the sugar in the water in a heavy-bottomed saucepan. Bring to a rapid simmer, watching carefully once most of the water has evaporated. It will start to caramelise at the edges, so shake and swirl the pan to keep the caramelisation even. Once the caramel is a shade darker than golden syrup, remove the pan from the heat and throw in a couple of tablespoons of water to stop further darkening. Add the miso paste and keep stirring until it cools down. Set aside until ready to use.

Preheat the oven to 190°C. Pat the chicken nibbles very dry. Brush with miso caramel so that every side is completely covered. Place in an oven dish and bake for 20 minutes. Remove from the oven, brush more caramel miso over the chicken and return to cook a few minutes longer until the chicken is a golden amber colour. Serve with an accompanying salad such as rocket, microgreens and cucumber ribbons.

Many cooks have a love/hate affair with offal. Top of my list of loves is chicken liver, with its dense texture and great flavour. Liver is a rich food so I like to temper it with plenty of acid to cut the powerful flavour. This recipe has two great sources of acid: apples and vinegar. The trick to cooking chicken livers is to sear them in a hot pan so the outsides are almost crisp and the interior is still pink and moist. This takes a little courage as chicken livers can explode in very hot oil. The apples and shallots slightly caramelise in the pan, and this dish makes a great starter or lunch for autumn when apples are at their best.

Chicken livers with shallots & apples

SERVES 4
WINE SUGGESTION: CABERNET SAUVIGNON OR MERLOT BLEND
BEST IN AUTUMN/WINTER

4 x 10cm squares puff pastry

1 egg yolk, beaten

8 shallots

350g chicken livers

2 apples

2 tbsp butter

1 tsp thyme leaves

6 tbsp Forum cabernet vinegar or any good red wine vinegar

½ cup chicken stock

1 lime, zest and juice

salt and freshly ground black pepper

2 tbsp parsley, finely chopped

Take the squares of puff pastry, score the tops and cut a small groove 1cm in on all sides. Glaze the tops with beaten egg yolk. Bake in a 200°C oven for 8–10 minutes until puffed and golden. Remove and keep aside.

Peel and trim the shallots. Trim the chicken livers and put aside.

Peel, core and slice the apples. Melt half the butter in a frying pan and add the shallots and apples with the thyme leaves. Cook very slowly until soft and golden. Remove the apples and shallots and place in a small bowl.

Deglaze the pan with the vinegar. Add the lime zest, juice and stock and simmer for a few minutes to reduce the liquid by half. Pour this sauce onto the reserved apples and shallots and put aside.

Add the remaining butter to the pan, turn up the heat and sauté the chicken livers fairly briskly so they brown nicely but remain slightly pink in the centre.

Return the apple and shallot mixture and sauce to the pan with the cooked chicken livers and reheat, seasoning to taste.

Reheat the pastry and with a sharp knife remove the centre of each square very carefully, so as not to break it. Spoon the seasoned, hot chicken livers and sauce into the warmed pastry cases and scatter the parsley over each dish. Top with the pastry lid and serve.

One of my favourite ways with any stone fruit is to grill it slowly over a charcoal barbecue. Cooking fruit helps to release the sugar within, so any under-ripe fruit will develop more flavour. Try to use firm nectarines rather than very ripe, squashy fruit for this lovely late-summer recipe as the heat will make them collapse quickly.

Roast chicken salad with nectarines & summer leaves

SERVES 6
WINE SUGGESTION: ROSÉ
BEST IN SUMMER/EARLY AUTUMN

1 size 16 free-range chicken

3 tbsp butter

¼ cup fresh tarragon leaves, chopped

salt and pepper

4 thick slices stale sourdough

2 tbsp extra virgin olive oil

6 ripe golden nectarines

1 large soft-leafed lettuce

1 small red onion, finely sliced

fresh basil leaves

For the dressing:

2 tbsp chardonnay or other white wine vinegar

4 tbsp extra virgin olive oil

salt and pepper

Preheat the oven to 200°C. Wipe the interior of the chicken with a paper towel. Put one tablespoon of butter in the cavity with a little of the tarragon and pepper and salt. Rub the skin with the remaining butter, scatter the remaining tarragon over the bird and season.

Roast the chicken for about 50 minutes or until the skin is golden and the juices run clear when the thigh is pierced with a skewer. Set aside to rest, reserving any juices from the pan.

Carve the chicken by cutting off the legs and thighs and dividing these between the joints. Remove each wing with a small slice of the breast. Cut the top half of the chicken away from the back and cut this into 5–6 portions. Remove the 'oysters' from the back, keeping the frame for chicken stock.

Prepare the sourdough nuggets by making rough pieces of bread of about 3cm. Toss the bread in the oil in a roasting pan then place in the oven for 15–20 minutes until crunchy and golden, tossing once or twice.

Halve the nectarines and remove the stones. Rub with a tiny amount of olive oil and place on a pre-heated ridged grill pan or hot barbecue to cook for no more than 3–4 minutes.

To assemble the salad, place the lettuce leaves on a platter. Arrange the chicken, sourdough nuggets, onion slices and grilled nectarines over the salad leaves, topping with the basil leaves. Mix the dressing ingredients together and pour over the salad with any reserved pan juices from the chicken. Serve at once.

The basis for a good, flavoursome chicken soup is to build it on the base of a tasty chicken stock. Chicken stock is not only a terrific standby in the refrigerator or freezer but also is one of the most rewarding and yet simple staples to make. It takes no time to assemble the basic ingredients: chicken bones or carcasses, a few vegetables – carrots, onion, celery – a bay leaf or two, parsley stalks, and some peppercorns. Throw these into a large saucepan, cover with cold water, bring to a simmer and allow the stock to bubble away for at least two hours, occasionally skimming any flotsam that rises to the top. Then it's a matter of passing the liquid through a sieve, and storing the stock in clean jars until needed. The fat that rises to the top and sets hard will help to keep the stock fresh for a week or two, if refrigerated.

Chicken & vegetable soup

SERVES 4–6
WINE SUGGESTION: SAUVIGNON BLANC
BEST IN ANY SEASON

1 size 16 free-range chicken

3 carrots, peeled and sliced

½ head of celery, sliced, some green leaves reserved

1 fennel bulb, sliced

6 sprigs fresh thyme

3 litres water

2 large handfuls thawed baby peas

egg noodles

1 small bunch fresh flat-leaf parsley, leaves picked

Wash the chicken under running cold water, then pat it dry, including the cavity, with kitchen paper. Place the whole chicken, carrots, celery, fennel and thyme into a large deep pan and pour in 3 litres of water or enough to cover the chicken.

Bring to a boil, turn down the heat and simmer over gentle heat for 60 minutes or until the chicken is cooked through. You can tell it is cooked when the tendons and skin on the legs start to pull away.

Using tongs, remove the chicken from the pan, taking care to tilt the chicken so any liquid inside the cavity spills back into the pot. Strain the broth into a clean pan or bowl, saving the vegetables on the side.

Return the broth to the rinsed-out pan, place over medium heat and allow to simmer until the broth is reduced by half. Meanwhile, once the chicken has cooled, remove all the meat from the bones, shredding the cooked chicken into long pieces and discarding the skin and bones.

When the broth has reduced, throw the vegetables back in the pan with the peas, egg noodles and shredded chicken meat. Simmer for a further 5 minutes, or until the noodles are cooked, then remove the sprigs of thyme.

Serve in warmed bowls with a sprinkling of chopped parsley and the reserved celery leaves.

You can purchase chicken mince for this recipe but I like to make my own by mincing chicken thigh meat – that way I know exactly what I am getting and there's no gristly or tough little bits to surprise me. Sourdough crumbs ensure that these delicious little dumplings are very tender, and are perfectly matched by the refreshing flavour combination of mint and lemon. You could always substitute another fresh green vegetable for the broad beans, such as asparagus spears, broccoli or French beans.

Chicken dumplings with braised broad beans, lemon & mint

SERVES 4
WINE SUGGESTION: CHARDONNAY
BEST IN SPRING

For the chicken dumplings:

1 onion, finely chopped

4 tbsp olive oil

6 boneless chicken thighs

½ cup sourdough crumbs

1 small egg

grated zest of 1 lemon

2 tbsp thyme leaves

pinch of smoked paprika

pinch of salt and freshly ground pepper

For the braised broad beans:

1kg broad beans

60ml extra virgin olive oil

1 onion, finely chopped

1 clove garlic, squashed

pinch of sugar and sea salt

300ml chicken stock

juice of 1 lemon

a small bunch of mint, finely chopped

To make the dumplings, put a tablespoon of the olive oil in a microwave bowl with the chopped onion and cook on full power for 2 minutes until soft and translucent.

Cut the chicken thighs into small chunks. Place in a food processor fitted with the sharp blade and process the chicken meat until finely minced. Add the cooked onion, sourdough crumbs, egg, lemon zest and thyme leaves with paprika, salt and pepper, and process until everything is well combined.

Remove the chicken mixture, wet your hands and roll into small golf-ball-sized dumplings.

Heat the remaining olive oil in a frying pan. Gently fry the chicken dumplings until they are just cooked through. Put aside.

To prepare the beans, remove them from the pods, place in a saucepan of boiling water and bring to a gentle simmer for 1–2 minutes. Refresh under cold water. Remove the skins of each bean by popping them out with your thumb and forefinger. Discard the skins.

Heat the oil in large frying pan and gently cook the onion until it is translucent. Add the garlic with a pinch of sugar and sea salt and cook for another minute. Add the stock with the beans and cooked dumplings and simmer for 3–4 minutes until heated through. Stir in the lemon juice and chopped mint and serve hot or cold.

This savoury chicken pie is cooked 'deep dish' style. The filling is piled into an ovenproof dish, topped and sealed with a pastry crust. While the pastry bakes, the filling reheats. It is important to use the best pastry that can be found, preferably made with butter, and the filling should have lots of flavour. The secret of any good savoury pie is to start with well-flavoured stock for the sauce.

Chicken, leek & bacon pie

SERVES 6 WITH A GREEN SALAD
WINE SUGGESTION: CHENIN BLANC
BEST IN AUTUMN/WINTER

To poach the chicken:

1 size 16–18 free-range chicken

1 stick celery, chopped

1 carrot, chopped

2 bay leaves

a handful of parsley stalks

For the pie filling:

50g butter

100g baby mushrooms, sliced

1 large leek, washed well and sliced

3 rashers streaky bacon, cut into thin strips

200ml full cream milk

1 bay leaf

2 tbsp flour

1 lemon, strips of zest only

2 tbsp fresh thyme leaves

150ml chicken stock

salt and pepper

250g ready-rolled flaky puff pastry

1 egg yolk, beaten

Place the chicken in a stockpot with the celery, carrot, bay leaves and parsley stalks and cover with cold water. Bring to the boil, reduce to simmer and allow the chicken to poach gently for 20 minutes. Turn the heat off and leave the chicken to stand in the hot liquid as it cools.

Once cool, remove the chicken from the pot and remove all the meat from the carcass. Put the meat aside in a clean bowl and return all the bones and skin to the pot. Simmer this for 2–3 hours to make a well-flavoured stock.

In a large saucepan, melt the butter and add the mushrooms, leeks and bacon. Cook over a gentle heat until the vegetables are soft and just starting to turn slightly golden.

Meanwhile put the milk in a small pan with the bay leaf, bring this to simmering point, then take off the heat to allow the bay leaf to infuse the milk.

Once the vegetables are softened, stir in the flour with the thyme leaves and lemon strips. Strain the hot milk and stir in with the measured chicken stock. Stir well over the heat until the sauce thickens. Add the reserved chicken meat, toss together gently and season to taste with salt and a generous pinch of black pepper.

Heat the oven to 200°C.

Allow the chicken mixture to cool, then pile it into an ovenproof pie dish (approx 30 x 20cm). Cover the top with the pastry, rolled to fit the dish. Brush the top with a little beaten egg and bake in the oven until the pastry is crisp and golden for about 30 minutes.

It's no surprise that lemons are almost always on every cook's list of favourite ingredients. The aromatic scent, the acidity that it adds to dishes, and the magical dimension it brings to food is why most cooks could not do without them. I keep a small bowl of fresh lemons in my kitchen, and preserved lemons, a Mediterranean specialty, are always in my fridge, ready to be chopped finely and added to casseroles, roasts, pies and so much more.

Casseroled chicken with fennel, potatoes, olives & preserved lemon

SERVES 6
WINE SUGGESTION: DRY RIESLING
BEST IN AUTUMN/WINTER/SPRING

12 free-range chicken legs, skin on

3 tbsp flour seasoned with salt and pepper

4 tbsp olive oil

1 onion, finely chopped

1 clove garlic, crushed

1 tsp ground ginger

6 small potatoes, cut into 2cm slices

2 halves preserved lemon, sliced into 4 pieces each, lengthwise

pinch of saffron, soaked in 2 tbsp hot water

4 small–medium fennel bulbs, sliced

500ml chicken stock

18 green olives

coriander sprigs for garnish

Preheat the oven to 180°C.

Wipe any extra water or juices from the legs, and dust lightly with flour, salt and pepper. Heat 2 tablespoons of the oil in a large frying pan and sauté the chicken until the skin is golden all over. Lift out and set aside.

Meanwhile in a heavy casserole dish suitable for stove-top use, heat the remaining oil. When hot, add the onion, garlic and ginger and cook gently until soft. Add the potato slices and continue cooking over a low heat for 2–3 minutes. Add the lemon, saffron and fennel, toss together well then add the stock, chicken and olives.

Bring this to a simmer, cover with a tightly fitting lid and bake in the oven for 45 minutes.

Remove from the oven and spoon the chicken, vegetables and olives onto a heated serving platter. Reduce the juices over a fast heat until they thicken and pour over the chicken. Garnish with a few coriander sprigs. Serve at once with a green salad or a plate of steamed broccoli.

Food Talk //
Which wine with that food?

We have a vibrant wine scene in New Zealand and our wines are desired in many countries, even those that make wine of their own. It makes sense to match local wines to the food that is grown here, and to support local winemakers. I like to consider regionality, so for me the best wine matches are when the food and the grapes have been grown in the same region. For example, seafood from the waters in the north of the South Island will go hand in hand with the fragrant white wines of that same terroir. Marlborough mussels or a light salmon dish with a local sauvignon blanc? Perfect.

An important factor in food and wine matching is what is known as the 'weight of the wine' – a light, mildly flavoured wine to match delicate, light food; a heavy, bold wine with muscular flavours to balance hearty rich food. As a rule, the simpler the food, the simpler the wine can be. Complexity is a wonderful thing but intense wine will overpower simple food, and a modest wine will be lost if your food has been built on a big flavour base, is filled with spices and other heady aromas, or is being served with an array of other tastes.

That complexity in wine and the tastes it carries should be considered when you're planning matches and cooking your food. The flavours and intensity of any wine is already captured in the bottle and there's no way you can change that (apart from rethinking and choosing a more suitable match). What you can do is alter or tweak the food you are cooking to suit the wine. Maybe the food needs a bit more brightness and lightness, which can be done by adding a little acidity like lemon juice to the food. Or if the wine is dark and broody, maybe your casserole needs more reduction to intensify the flavour, or more salt so all the complex notes in the food can be tasted. Maybe you could add another side dish that acts as a foil to the main dish.

If the food is light and aromatic it will go well with aromatic wines like riesling, pinot gris, gewürztraminer or one of the European varietals such as albariño or grüner veltliner that are becoming more prevalent and recently planted here in New Zealand. As soon as you introduce a creamy or rich sauce you will need to think about offering a slightly heavier chardonnay or a chenin blanc. You can serve red wine with light food but it should be fresh and lively like a young pinot noir or a Beaujolais-style wine.

Once winter sets in, heavy food, long slow cooking and roasting means bringing out the more muscular wines like syrah or cabernet blend. If you're a white wine fan, a heavier, richer chardonnay can also be served as it's often powerful enough to maintain its strength with most hearty food and meat. A rich fish stew or a meaty tuna dish can go with red wine too, but take care the wine is not too complex.

In terms of dessert, there's not a lot of choice. Wines need to be sweeter than the dessert they accompany. You will get a sour taste in your wine if it is not sweeter than your pudding. Wines labelled 'late harvest' are likely to be sweet as the grapes have hung onto the vines for much longer to develop higher sugar. But if you can't find a sweet wine to suit, serve the wine with cheese rather than dessert.

Another point to remember is the serving temperature. White wines mostly, but not always, should be slightly chilled, while red wines need to be served at room temperature. In really hot weather you should slightly chill the reds. And if you're lucky enough to have genuine champagne, it should always be served chilled.

Some wines make wonderful aperitifs. They are generally aromatic wines like sauvignon blanc, riesling and gewürztraminer that can stand on their own, and maybe paired with light cocktail food.

And importantly, consider experimenting with the new wine varietals and with unusual matches. There's a wonderful world of wine out there. It can be quite illuminating to try wines from different vintages, observing what effect the weather and cellaring can have on flavours and weight in any wine from year to year.

My mother spoiled us in our early years by cooking a plump roast chicken for special occasions. Chicken was a rare treat back then, yet Mum always managed to come up trumps. She would pour her love into roasting that bird, stuffing it with all sorts of savoury goodness and serving up an aromatic gravy made from the pan juices.

The ultimate roast chicken

SERVES 4–6
WINE SUGGESTION: CHARDONNAY
BEST IN ANY SEASON

1.6kg free-range chicken

2 tbsp softened butter

4 tbsp chopped fresh herbs (parsley, mint)

1 tsp salt

freshly ground black pepper

½ cup chicken stock

To finish:

3 thick slices stale sourdough

1 tbsp chopped preserved lemon

4 tbsp sliced mint

1 tsp ground cumin

Preheat the oven to 180°C.

Wash the chicken under cold water inside and out. Dry thoroughly with paper towels. Mix the butter and herbs with a little of the salt and some pepper to form a paste. Gently work your fingers underneath the skin, separating it from the flesh without tearing or puncturing, and push the butter all over the breast of the chicken and down towards the leg joints. Smooth and tease it out, with any remaining butter pushed into the cavity.

Place the chicken in a roasting pan breast-side up, and sprinkle remaining salt over it. Pour the stock into the pan, and roast for an hour, basting two or three times while it roasts. (You can place potato, kumara, pumpkin, parsnip or beetroot around the chicken to roast in the juices.) Check the chicken is cooked by piercing the thigh with a knife. The juices should run clear.

Remove the chicken from the oven when cooked and place on a warmed platter. Cover with foil and a tea towel and rest it for 10–15 minutes. This allows the juices to become reabsorbed, producing succulent meat. Meanwhile, break the sourdough into chunks and throw into the roasting pan on a heated element on the stovetop so the juices bubble and are absorbed into the bread. Add the preserved lemon, mint and cumin and toss well. Cook until the bread becomes crisp.

Carve the chicken into pieces, return them to the warm platter and strew the bread and juices around and over the top. Serve with roast vegetables and steamed broccoli.

Poussins (baby chickens) make an ideal treat for a special dinner and can be ordered through most butchers and good supermarkets. The larger-sized poussins are worth seeking if you wish to split these birds in two. I prefer to buy the smaller birds (less than 350g) to serve a whole bird for each of my guests. This is a lovely end-of-season dish to make in autumn when the parsley in the garden is starting to dry out and the seed heads and stalks can be used, bringing lots of extra flavour.

Poussins with pears & parsley

SERVES 4
WINE SUGGESTION: PINOT GRIS
BEST IN LATE SUMMER/AUTUMN

4 poussins

60g butter

rind and juice of 1 lemon

3 fresh pears

salt and freshly ground black pepper

5 or 6 dried parsley stalks

2 cups pear cider (known as Perry)

extra butter

Preheat the oven to 200°C.

Wash and dry the poussins carefully as the skin is very delicate. Melt the butter to brush the skins of each bird. Lay the birds in a roasting pan and grate the lemon rind over them.

Quarter and core the pears and nestle them amongst the poussins. Season generously with salt and pepper. Pour the pear cider and lemon juice into the roasting pan and place the parsley stalks on top.

Cook in the preheated oven for about 25 minutes or until the skin is crispy and golden brown and the juice of the poussins runs clear when tested with a skewer.

Remove from the oven, rest the poussins for 5 minutes and then serve on individual plates with the pears and a little of the pan juices poured over. Serve with steamed green beans and braised carrots tossed in extra butter.

'Tray bakes' have become enormously popular as meat, vegetables and some nice flavourings are packed into an oven dish or tray and baked in the oven to make a complete meal – such an easy dinner solution. The art of a good tray bake, however, is making sure all those ingredients need the same amount of cooking time. In this recipe, the chicken, fennel and potatoes will take the same time to cook, but the apricots if quite ripe will collapse and go mushy, so add them halfway or later in the baking time.

Tray-baked chicken with potatoes & apricots

SERVES 4–6
WINE SUGGESTION: CHARDONNAY
BEST IN SUMMER/EARLY AUTUMN

1 chicken (or 4 leg and thigh portions)

2 tsp dried oregano

1 tsp sumac

½ tsp chilli flakes

sea salt

1 tbsp honey

4 tbsp olive oil

4 medium potatoes

1 small bulb fennel

5 cloves garlic

1 lemon

8 apricots

small bunch of fresh mint

2 tbsp chopped preserved lemon

If using a whole chicken, cut it into neat portions – cut the thigh and legs off and then separate the leg from the thigh. Cut off the wings with a good chunk of the breast. Cut the remaining breast meat into two or three large portions. Alternatively use legs and thighs and cut each into two pieces. You should have eight or nine portions.

Mix the oregano, sumac, chilli flakes, honey, salt and olive oil together and place in a shallow dish or a sealable plastic bag. Add the chicken portions and turn well to coat with this marinade. Refrigerate overnight or for at least two hours.

Preheat the oven to 200°C.

Cut each potato into four neat chunks. Slice the fennel, discarding the centre core. Leave the garlic unpeeled. Slice the lemon into wedges and cut the apricots in half, removing the stones.

Place all the vegetables except the apricots in a large roasting pan. Place the marinated chicken pieces on top, pushing them down a little so they mingle with the vegetables and sprinkle the salt over everything.

Roast for about 30 minutes, taking the dish out a couple of times to baste everything with the juices that form. Add the apricots, pushing them into the pan juices under the chicken and continue to bake for about 15 minutes, until the chicken is golden brown and everything is crisp. Remove from the oven.

Sprinkle mint leaves and the chopped preserved lemon over the dish and serve accompanied by a fresh green salad.

This tray bake is perfect for colder weather when leeks and pumpkin are in abundance. When using whole leeks, trim the roots away without completely cutting off the base so that the leek holds together. The top dark, coarse leaves should be trimmed neatly and discarded; with smaller leeks, they will only need a little trimming of any tatty tops. If slicing leeks, cut them through with a sharp knife on the diagonal as they look more attractive than straight slices.

Baked chicken, leek & pumpkin

SERVES 4–6
WINE SUGGESTION: CHARDONNAY
BEST IN AUTUMN/WINTER

1 organic free-range chicken, butterflied

sea salt and freshly ground black pepper

3 leeks, well washed

300g pumpkin, peeled and cut into 5cm chunks

½ cup green olives

1 tbsp preserved lemon, flesh discarded and rind cut into tiny dice

½ cup rosemary or thyme leaves, stripped from the stalks

4 tbsp extra virgin olive oil

2 tbsp good-quality balsamic vinegar

Preheat the oven to 200°C.

Prepare the chicken by patting it dry and dusting with salt and pepper on all sides.

Cut the leeks into 5cm chunks and place in a roasting dish with the pumpkin pieces. Toss the vegetables with the olives, preserved lemon dice, herb leaves, salt and pepper, olive oil and balsamic until well mixed. Tip them into a roasting pan and sit the chicken on top.

Place in the oven and roast for 45 minutes, checking occasionally and shaking the pan so it all cooks evenly. When the chicken is fragrant and thoroughly cooked (you can pierce the thigh and make sure the juices run clear) remove the pan from the oven and cover immediately with foil. Stack a couple of tea towels on top and allow to stand for 10 minutes so the juices set.

Transfer the vegetables to a large serving platter, and cut the chicken into portions.

Serve immediately, or if serving later, place in a covered dish and refrigerate until needed. Serve hot or at room temperature.

Duck is one of my favourite meats but like most cooks it rarely appears on my plate. Somehow it always seems difficult to deal with, but this recipe and the following one are not complex. The meaty breasts are the easiest and quickest way to get a duck dinner on the table, as they can be cooked in a heavy frying pan in less than 15 minutes. There's a significant layer of fat on a duck, so always start the cooking process of duck breasts skin-side down in a cold frying pan, so the maximum amount of fat is released. Don't tip the fat away; keep it covered in the refrigerator for another use such as roasting potatoes or frying vegetables. The results are truly delicious.

Three-bean salad with lemon & sliced duck breast

SERVES 4 AS AN ENTRÉE
WINE SUGGESTION: RIESLING
BEST IN SPRING

300g tender young green beans

15 pods of broad beans

1 cup or can preserved white butter beans

2 duck breasts

salt and freshly ground black pepper

For the dressing:

1 lemon, grated zest and juice

6 tbsp grapeseed oil

salt and freshly ground pepper

herb flowers for garnish

Prepare the vegetables. Blanch the beans in boiling salted water for 2 minutes, drain and immediately plunge into a bowl of ice-cold water.

Remove the broad beans from their pods and blanch in boiling salted water. Cool and slip the outer skin from the beans.

Remove the white beans from the jar or can and rinse under cold water.

Score the skin from the duck breasts and sprinkle generously with salt and pepper. Place, skin-side down, in a cold frying pan. Put the pan over the heat, and gently cook for 10 minutes until the skin is crisp and golden. Turn and cook the second side of each for 3 minutes, remove from the pan and allow the meat to rest for 7–10 minutes.

Make a dressing by whisking the lemon juice, oil and salt and pepper together.

Scatter the beans over the serving plates. Slice each duck breast into six pieces and place them on top of the beans.

Pour a little dressing over each plate and add a few spring herb flowers and some freshly grated lemon zest for decoration.

Duck leg portions need slower, longer cooking than the breast portions. I love slow-cooked duck ragout like this one where the duck legs are cooked briefly, meat removed from the bone and then gently simmered in a rich ragout to make a tasty sauce for pasta. A little meat goes a long way in this recipe, which would work well with both farmed duckling and wild duck meat.

Duck & mandarin ragout

SERVES 4
WINE MATCH: A FRUITY RIESLING
BEST IN WINTER/SPRING

2 duck legs

salt and pepper

5 tbsp olive oil

1 small onion, finely chopped

1 carrot, peeled and diced

2 stalks celery, finely diced

several sprigs fresh thyme

3 mandarins

150ml riesling

1 litre chicken stock

150g egg pappardelle noodles

parsley and Grana Padano cheese for garnish

Season the duck with pepper and salt. Heat a heavy frying pan with 2 tablespoons of the olive oil, and when hot, add the duck legs. Lower the heat and cook, turning frequently until cooked through with golden crisp skin. Remove and cool slightly.

Meanwhile begin the ragout sauce. Put the remaining oil in a saucepan. Add the onion, carrot and celery and cook over a low heat for about 10–15 minutes until it is all soft and golden. Add the grated zest and juice of two of the mandarins, with the thyme, riesling and chicken stock. Bring to a gentle simmer for 20 minutes.

Pull all the duck meat from the bones, add the meat to the pan and simmer a further 15 or 20 minutes until the meat is tender and the sauce reduced by half.

Cook the pasta in a large pot of boiling salted water until it is al dente or just soft. Drain and toss the ragout through.

Peel the remaining mandarin and chop into segments.

To serve, divide between four plates and garnish with freshly chopped parsley and the mandarin pieces. Hand around the grated cheese separately.

SECTION 6

Sweet as...

190 Fresh apricot & ricotta tart
192 Blueberry syllabub
194 Strawberry & crème fraîche tartlets
196 *Food Talk: Dessert is on the table*
200 Chocolate cupcakes with salted caramel sauce
202 Lemon delicious
204 Raspberry & chocolate meringue tangle
206 Caramelised rhubarb & apple tart with compote
208 Griestorte with fresh strawberries
210 Chocolate meringues with chocolate cream
212 Pear & almond croissant pudding
214 Lemon posset with mandarin
216 Coconut & rosewater rice puddings with strawberries
218 Spanish cream with berries
220 Frosted brown sugar cookies
222 Fig & honey clafoutis

There's a world of difference between fruit picked locally, sweet and ripe from the tree, and the fruit that has been plucked while still green in order to join the supermarket distribution network. I love ripe stone fruit that's heavily scented and juicy enough to dribble down my chin as I take a bite but it's rare to find that. Transported fruit is best for cooking in tarts and cakes, gently stewing or for jam and chutney making. This apricot tart is one of my favourites but make sure the fruit you use is not overripe.

Fresh apricot & ricotta tart

SERVES 8
WINE SUGGESTION: LATE-HARVEST RIESLING
BEST IN SUMMER

500g flaky puff pastry

400g ricotta

1 lemon, zest and juice

2 tbsp caster sugar

½ tsp ground cinnamon

1kg fresh ripe apricots

3 tbsp sliced almonds

6 tbsp apricot jam

3 tbsp water

Roll the pastry out to fit a 20 x 30cm tart tin, then ease it in so the pastry just overlaps the edges of the tin. Prick the surface with a fork. Allow the pastry to rest for 30 minutes before filling with the ricotta and fruit.

Preheat the oven to 200°C.

Tip the ricotta into a bowl and add the lemon zest and juice, caster sugar and cinnamon. Beat well and spread this mixture into the pastry case.

Cut the apricots in half, remove the stones and place them cut-side down on the ricotta. Sprinkle the almonds between the apricots.

Place the tart in the oven, reduce the heat to 180°C and bake for 40 minutes or until the pastry is golden and crisp. Remove from the oven.

Combine the apricot jam and water and melt over gentle heat. Using a pastry brush, paint this hot jam onto the top of the apricots and make sure to fill any crevices.

Serve with Greek-style yogurt or whipped cream.

Blueberries, almost unknown in New Zealand a couple of decades ago, have been enjoying their time in the sun as a very healthy and trendy fruit. They are lovely fresh, perfect for decoration, and seem to make an appearance on every breakfast fruit platter. They're delicious and tangy and can be used to make a light syllabub-like fresh fruit mousse. If you'd prefer to use yogurt rather than whipped cream, that's fine, but be sure to choose a thick, unsweetened and unflavoured Greek yogurt.

Blueberry syllabub

SERVES 8 IN SMALL GLASSES
WINE SUGGESTION: A SMALL GLASS OF FRUITY LIQUEUR OR BRANDY
BEST IN EVERY SEASON

375g blueberries, fresh or frozen

75g caster sugar

300ml cream, plus extra whipped cream for decoration

2 tbsp brandy

lemon juice to taste

For decoration:

a handful of fresh blueberries

Amaretti biscuits

Gently simmer the blueberries and sugar together until the fruit collapses (about 3–4 minutes). Strain the purée through a fine sieve and allow to cool in a large bowl.

Using a hand-held electric beater, whisk the purée with the cream and brandy until the mixture thickens. Adjust the flavour with a little lemon juice to taste and refrigerate until ready to serve.

To serve, spoon the syllabub into individual glass dishes, and add some fresh blueberries. Top with roughly chopped Amaretti biscuits.

These tartlets should be eaten the same day, although they are so good there's perhaps no need to say this as they're bound to disappear fast. Crème fraîche is a cultured cream with a thick consistency and a delicious tang to it. It holds its shape and is thick enough to last for hours without weeping any excess moisture. If you cannot find any, replace it with a thick sour cream. You can also make these little tartlets with other fruit – raspberries, blueberries, slices of stone fruits or passionfruit. Apricot jam makes a great glaze in place of strawberry jam

Strawberry & crème fraîche tartlets

MAKES 12 TARTLETS. RECIPE CAN BE SCALED UP.
WINE SUGGESTION: SPARKLING ROSÉ
BEST IN SPRING /SUMMER

For the pastry:

120g cold unsalted butter

180g flour

pinch of salt

4 tbsp water (approx)

For the filling:

150g strawberry jam

150g crème fraîche (Zany Zeus)

12 smallish strawberries

To make the pastry, chop the butter into small pieces and place in the food processor with the flour and the salt. Turn the motor on and run until the butter and flour are a sandy consistency. Add a few drops of water and pulse the mixture, adding enough water so the pastry starts to come together and form 'crumbs'. Tip this out onto a clean bench and knead lightly to form a ball. Chill for about 30 minutes.

To cook the pastry, preheat the oven to 160°C. Roll the pastry out on a floured board and then cut circles slightly larger than the tartlet tins. Using floured fingers, ease the pastry into each of the tins. Let the pastry chill for about 30 minutes in the fridge. Line each of the tartlet shells with crushed baking paper and fill with baking beans. (Raw rice will work but won't be reusable except for 'baking blind'.)

Bake the pastry cases in the oven for about 10 minutes until pale golden. Remove the beans or rice and paper. When cool, spoon half a teaspoon of jam into the bottom of each tartlet.

Beat the crème fraîche with a fork or small whisk so it is soft and pliable. Spoon a teaspoonful or two on top of the jam. Slice the strawberries and place two or three slices on each tart.

Melt the remaining strawberry jam and brush while hot over the strawberries for a glossy finish.

Food Talk //
Dessert is on the table

For me the best puddings involve fruit. I grew up in a household where my mother always served a dessert or pudding each night. I have fond memories of vanilla ice cream with hot chocolate sauce, lovely hot jam rolls with custard, chocolate log, baked or steamed puddings that involved golden syrup and of course gorgeous seasonal or preserved fruit. If all else failed there would be one of the many jars of golden queen peaches she had spent hours peeling, slicing and bottling.

We are lucky in New Zealand to have fresh fruit available year round, and for the most part fruit that's grown in almost all regions of the country. The past generations of Kiwis had what was known as the quarter-acre paradise, a reference to homes that were surrounded by lawns, gardens and fruit trees. As the majority of the population moved to the cities, demand on land has meant housing has become denser, and not as many folk have direct access to those lemon, plum, apple, feijoa and other backyard trees that were so loved.

Commercial growers and imports now mean we can lose sight of which fruit are in their prime season or what is local. A trip to a specialist fruit-and-vegetable shop will give more clues as to what is in season than supermarkets who strive to make everything available all year round. We should take advantage of and celebrate our local, seasonal fruit.

The spring fruits we love are strawberries, blackberries, raspberries, varieties of orange and the very first cherries. Then the stone fruit season arrives with Christmas and the first signs of summer. Plums, cherries, apricots, nectarines, peaches and some of the more unusual stone fruits like plumcots, pluots and flattos are in abundance from late December through to March.

Next in the fresh fruit scene are the pip fruits – a vast selection of cooking and eating apples, and varieties of pears that range from cooking pears to fragrant, juicy eating pears, nashi pears and quince. These fruit are closely followed by autumnal fruits. Figs are first, usually arriving with the first of the outdoor grapes, then there's persimmon, feijoa, kiwifruit, tamarillos, and cherry guavas.

Finally, just as winter sets in, our citrus crop starts to ripen, with mandarins, oranges, limes and lemons to stave off the coughs and colds and provide a wealth of great tastes to incorporate into puddings and desserts.

Sometimes friends consult me when they need a dessert for a dinner they're organising. My standard answer is to make things easy by offering a fresh fruit salad, served with ice cream, whipped cream, yogurt or a combination of all these things. My philosophy is that diners need to end a meal with something easy to eat and easy to digest. Fruit is brilliantfor this.

Of course there's always the essential big three Cs of dessert, too: chocolate, caramel and custard. To combine any of these three with seasonal fruit will create a winning dessert.

FRUIT SALAD

When making fresh fruit salad, there are two approaches to take. Either keep it really simple by using a combination of just two or three fruits in season, such as apricots, cherries and blueberries, or feijoa, persimmon and kiwifruit, or go for a little of everything you can find.

We import some lovely exotic fruits from our neighbours in the Pacific, so I often start with a fresh mango, papaya or pineapple and cut it into bite-sized pieces. I will then add the other fruits in season, allowing about a cup of cut-up fruit per person and always thinking about providing a variety of colours. And it doesn't matter if you make more than you need as leftovers can go in the fridge for serving next morning at breakfast.

There's no need to drown everything in sugar as fruit naturally has a built-in combination of fructose (fruit sugars) and acidity that helps to cleanse the palate. I do add juice of half a lemon and a tablespoon or two of vanilla syrup or maple syrup to toss through the fruit. If you must, you can add a slosh of sweet white wine, or a jig or two of a liqueur if there are no kiddies around. Serve chilled with custard, whipped cream or yogurt.

It's worth mastering the art of a rich pouring custard made with egg yolks and creamy milk, flavoured with real vanilla. There's no substitute for this unctuous sauce when it is made properly. Here are two variations on custard that I love to make, the classic version and a coconut custard.

Classic custard

3 egg yolks

90g sugar

300ml milk

1 vanilla bean

To make the custard, beat together the egg yolks and sugar until light and thick. Heat the milk with the vanilla bean in a heavy-based saucepan until it almost comes to the boil. Tip the hot milk on to the egg mixture in a bowl and stir well to combine. Rinse the pan that the milk was heated in, return to the heat and strain the egg, sugar and milk mixture into the pan. Carefully reheat the custard, stirring constantly until the mixture thickens and coats the spoon. It's important not to let this boil as the mixture will curdle. If it even starts to curdle around the edges, remove it immediately from the heat and whisk vigorously until it is smooth again. Allow the custard to cool and refrigerate until needed.

Coconut custard

400ml coconut cream

3 free-range egg yolks

2 tbsp soft brown sugar

2 tsp cornflour

Pour the coconut milk into a heavy-bottomed pan. Place over gentle heat. Stir and bring to simmering point: do not allow it to boil. Remove from the heat. Meanwhile, beat the yolks, sugar and cornflour together in a large heatproof bowl. Pour the hot cream mixture onto the yolk and sugar mixture, stirring vigorously as you do so. Rinse the pan, turn the heat right down, and pour the custard back into the pan. Stir continuously over a very gentle heat until the custard coats the back of your wooden spoon. It may take some time, so have a cup of tea handy. Decant into a jug and press plastic wrap on to the surface to prevent skin forming. Can be served warm or cold.

Serves 6

CARAMEL NOTES

It is almost a culinary art to make a good caramel. Once you have mastered the basics you will be able to produce either a creamy or clear caramel syrup, or the crunchy caramel toffee that you can chop up and use as a sweet garnish on desserts and cakes. Caramel can be tricky as it is made by heating dissolved sugar until it reaches the temperature where it starts to turn a golden colour. The danger is that the caramel, once it reaches the point where the sugar turns from being just liquid sugar into the golden, almost syrupy stage, is extremely hot and could cause a nasty burn if it touches any skin. It also can be very patchy, almost burning in places if it is not cooking evenly. But caramel is a great technique to master, so here are some tips to help:

- Use a heavy-based pan as a thin saucepan will not allow the sugar to dissolve and cook evenly or steadily.

- You can make caramel in any quantity but it's best to start with about ½ cup sugar with enough water to dissolve the crystals completely – roughly about half a cup. Always dissolve the sugar completely before bringing the syrup to the boil.

- Any sugar crystals clinging to the sides of the saucepan will not dissolve and will burn, so use a small brush to push them down before the syrup comes to the boil.

- Once the sugar is boiling it will reach a very high heat (over 170°C) and become dangerously hot. To prevent burns, keep your hands well clear of the pan and make sure children are not in the kitchen.

- Take the caramel off the stove immediately it reaches a golden colour. It can turn dark brown and burn very quickly.

- If you want shards of caramel or would like to coat fruit or anything else in solid caramel, do not add water or cream. Have an oiled tray ready or baking paper and use the caramel once it reaches the golden colour. It will set straight away as it cools so do not leave this task until you have finished.

- When adding water or cream to make a sauce or syrup, remove the pan and work carefully as any spitting from the pan will result in burns.

- The caramel will mass into a solid form when the water or cream hits it, so return the pan over a low heat and stir it gently until that mass dissolves.

- Caramel sauce will keep indefinitely in the refrigerator and may solidify. Bring it to room temperature to soften.

These lovely little cupcakes will be loved by both kids and adults alike. They are made with a delicious chocolate-cake mixture, and then topped with cream and drizzled with salted caramel. See the notes (on the previous page) on caramel before you begin, and if you have any caramel left over, store it in the fridge to use on another dessert or cake. It is delicious drizzled over ice cream.

Chocolate cupcakes with salted caramel sauce

SERVES 12
WINE SUGGESTION: CHOCOLATE LIQUEUR
BEST IN ALL SEASONS

100g caster sugar

125g soft brown sugar

3 large eggs

175ml sunflower oil

1 tsp vanilla extract

190g self-raising flour

60g cocoa powder

2 tsp baking powder

175ml full cream milk

Salted caramel sauce:

400g sugar

½ cup water

500ml cream

½ tsp salt

Preheat the oven to 160°C. Grease a 12-cup muffin/cupcake tray with butter, then sprinkle lightly with flour and set aside.

Place the sugar, eggs, oil and vanilla in the bowl of an electric mixer or use an electric hand-mixer and whisk well until it becomes pale, fluffy and aerated.

Sieve the flour, cocoa and baking powder together and gently whisk into the mixture. Finally add the milk to create a fairly thin cake batter. Pour into the prepared tins and bake for around 30 minutes until a skewer inserted into the cakes comes out clean. Allow to cool for at least 10 minutes in the tin before turning the cakes out onto a wire rack to finish cooling.

To make the salted caramel sauce, put the sugar and water into a heavy-based saucepan. Place the pan over gentle heat and dissolve the sugar before the syrup comes to a simmer. Allow the syrup to boil at steady rate, watching carefully (see 'Food Talk' on caramel). Once it is a rich golden colour, remove the pan from the heat and pour in 250ml of cream. Return the pan to the heat and gently stir the caramel, adding the salt, until it is smooth and creamy. Transfer to a heatproof bowl and refrigerate once it cools.

To serve, cut the top off each cake. Whip the remaining cream and put a spoonful in each cake. Pour over the chilled caramel sauce and replace the tops on the cakes.

I grew up in a home where the family dinner table was beautifully set every night (usually by me) and my mother made a dessert or pudding daily for us. When lemons are plentiful it's the ideal time to serve this classic dessert she often made. Lemon Delicious, a baked lemon self-saucing pudding, is a thing of wonder. A crust forms on top during baking, with a gorgeously acidic sponge beneath that hides the thick lemony custard in the bottom of the dish. Make sure you dig in to give everyone a little of each of the layers, and serve it with whipped cream, just like my mother always has.

Lemon delicious

SERVES 6
DRINKS SUGGESTION: LIMONCELLO
BEST IN LATE AUTUMN/WINTER

50g butter

200g sugar

4 eggs, separated

4 tbsp self-raising flour

330ml milk

grated rind and juice of 2 juicy lemons (about half a cup)

Preheat the oven to 170°C. Butter an ovenproof dish or soufflé dish (about 2-litre capacity).

Melt the butter in a bowl and using an electric hand-held whisk, beat in the sugar and egg yolks until the mixture is thick and creamy.

Sift the flour into the mixture, and carefully stir in with the milk, the lemon rind and juice.

Beat the egg whites in a clean bowl until stiff, fold them into the mixture and pile into the greased soufflé dish.

Stand the dish in a larger shallow dish filled with hot water. Bake in the oven for about 50 minutes until the spongy top is pale gold and firm. Accompany with whipped cream or yogurt.

I love the magical raspberry and chocolate combination so much that I have used it as a variation on the wonderful English classic, Eton Mess. You can make the crisp meringues and the chocolate sauce a day or two ahead but do not assemble the final dish until about 2 or 3 hours before serving. It is probably my favourite dessert of all time and one I serve over and over again.

Raspberry & chocolate meringue tangle

SERVES 8
WINE SUGGESTION: SPARKLING ROSÉ
BEST IN SUMMER

For the meringues:

4 egg whites

220g sugar

½ tsp pure vanilla essence

40g crushed freeze-dried raspberries ('Fresh As' brand from good grocery & speciality stores)

For the chocolate sauce:

200ml cream

200g finest-quality dark chocolate

50g soft brown sugar

To finish:

300ml cream

300ml Greek-style yogurt

3 punnets mixed berries: raspberries, strawberries and blueberries

Preheat the oven to 150°C. Line a baking tray with baking paper. Using an electric beater whisk the egg whites until stiff. Add the sugar a little at a time, continuing to beat and add the vanilla essence. Remove the beater-head and fold in the freeze-dried raspberries. Spoon small tablespoons of the meringue mixture onto the baking tray, leaving a gap between each meringue. Bake the meringues for one hour, then turn the oven off and leave to cool. Makes about 24. Store in an airtight tin for up to a week. Take a medium saucepan and half fill with water. Sit a large heatproof bowl over the saucepan so that it fits snugly with the base above the water line. Bring the water to the boil and reduce the heat so the water is barely simmering.

Place the cream, chocolate and sugar in the bowl, and stir for about 3 minutes or until chocolate almost melts. Remove the bowl from the heat and continue to stir until all the chocolate melts. You do not want the chocolate to 'seize' or turn grainy. Place this chocolate sauce in a dry airtight jar. Will keep in the fridge for 3–4 weeks. Serve at room temperature or reheat very carefully in a small bowl over simmering water.

Whip the cream until soft but not too stiff and fold in the yogurt, in a very large bowl. Break up about 1 dozen meringues into 2–3 pieces and add to the creamy mixture with most of the berries. Fold gently so everything is just combined but not swamped. Serve with the remaining berries and a drizzle of the chocolate sauce over the top.

Rhubarb grows almost year round in New Zealand gardens and is often regarded as an old-fashioned, almost forgotten fruit. It is sweet when young, developing more acidity as the stalks thicken and age. Look for rhubarb with the large leaves still attached, indicating it is fresh. Discard the leaves, and pull off any of those crisp brown bits found at the bottom of the stalk where it has been snapped from the crown it has grown from. If you have a surfeit of rhubarb stalks, cut them into small pieces, pack them into sealable plastic bags and store them in the fridge for up to a week, or pop them in the freezer. Rhubarb is delicious when gently stewed with a little sugar or honey.

Caramelised rhubarb & apple tart with compote

SERVES 6
WINE SUGGESTION: LATE-HARVEST RIESLING
BEST IN ALL SEASONS

500g sheet pre-rolled puff pastry

2 apples, peeled and cored

2 stems rhubarb

100g cream cheese

zest of 1 lemon

4 tbsp dark brown sugar

4 tbsp redcurrant jelly for glazing

12 walnut halves

Rhubarb compote with pomegranate syrup & ginger

4 stems of rhubarb, washed and trimmed

2 tbsp caster sugar

3 tbsp water

2 tbsp pomegranate syrup

3 or 4 pieces crystallised ginger cut into fine slices

Preheat the oven to 200°C. Ease the puff pastry into a rectangular 12 x 30cm, or a 22cm-round, loose-bottomed tart tin. Quarter the apples and slice each piece into 4–5 slices. Slice the rhubarb neatly. Spread the cream cheese over the pastry and sprinkle with the lemon zest. Arrange the apple and rhubarb slices in neat rows and sprinkle with the sugar and walnuts.

Bake for 20–25 minutes until the fruit is soft and slightly caramelised and the pastry is golden and puffed. Melt the jelly and with a pastry brush glaze the liquid over the fruit as it cools.

For the compote, slice the rhubarb neatly and place in a saucepan with the sugar and water. Bring to a simmer, cover with the lid and allow to cook gently for 5 minutes until soft.

As it cools, stir in the pomegranate syrup and the ginger. Refrigerate until needed. This is also delicious served over vanilla ice cream.

Serve a thin slice of the tart with a little cream and the compote.

Everyone loves a sponge cake and this recipe, a variation on a classic sponge, is one I added to my repertoire back in my days at the London Cordon Bleu School. The fine semolina gives the cake a delicate texture and there's far more flavour than most sponges as the lemon and almond add their distinct aromas. Serve this cake for afternoon tea or as a feather-light dessert.

Griestorte with fresh strawberries

SERVES 8
WINE SUGGESTION: ASTI SPUMANTE
BEST IN SPRING/SUMMER

4 eggs

180g caster sugar

2 small lemons, grated zest and juice

90g fine semolina

2 tbsp ground almonds

300ml cream

1 punnet strawberries, tops removed and sliced

Preheat the oven to 160°C. Prepare a 22cm cake tin by buttering the sides, lining the base with a disc of baking paper, buttering again, and dusting with caster sugar and flour.

Separate the eggs. Beat the yolks and sugar together in an electric cake mixer until thick and mousse-like. Add the lemon zest and juice and continue beating until the mixture forms a ribbon when lifted with a spoon. Carefully stir in the semolina and ground almonds with a metal spoon.

Whisk the egg whites until they form peaks, then gently fold them into the mixture. Spoon the batter immediately into the prepared tin and bake for 30–40 minutes. It should be golden and a skewer inserted in the middle of the cake should come out clean.

When the cake is cool, pile the whipped cream on top and cover with the sliced strawberries.

These meringues are irresistible, so rich and chocolatey with their creamy chocolate filling. The technique of the perfect meringue is getting the balance of sugar to egg-white exact, so take care to measure accurately. An electric beater is essential to ensure the mixture becomes thick and shiny, as using a rotary beater or a balloon whisk will take forever.

Chocolate meringues with chocolate cream

MAKES 15–20 FINISHED MERINGUES
WINE SUGGESTION: CHAMPAGNE
BEST IN ALL SEASONS

For the meringues:

3 egg whites

180g caster sugar

2 tbsp cocoa powder

3 tbsp grated chocolate

For the chocolate cream

100g dark chocolate

50ml double cream

Preheat the oven to 140°C. Beat the egg whites in an electric beater until they form stiff peaks. Gradually add the sugar, a spoonful at a time, and continue whisking.

When the mixture is puffed, smooth and glossy, remove the bowl and with a large metal spoon, stir in the cocoa and chocolate, taking care not to lose volume.

Line a large baking tray with baking paper and place or pipe the mixture in dollops, the size of golf balls. Make sure the meringues are well spaced. Bake for 50 minutes. The outside should be crisp. Turn the heat off and allow the meringues to stand in the oven for an hour or even longer. This will help the insides to set.

Place on a cake rack to dry out and cool. Store in an airtight tin until ready to use.

Makes 30–40.

For the chocolate cream break the chocolate into small pieces and place in a small heavy-bottomed saucepan with the cream. Place over gentle heat until the chocolate just melts. Stir, but be careful not to overdo it as this will cause the chocolate to seize or split. Pour into a bowl and cool in the refrigerator until it is thick and cold.

Take a heaped teaspoonful of the chocolate, spread over one meringue and then press a second meringue down so the two join together.

This dessert is a stunning variation of bread-and-butter pudding, made with sliced almond-filled croissants. Traditionally, French bakers would stuff almond paste into their leftover croissants, and rebake them for sale next day, but they have become such a popular item they are now freshly baked, daily. Add lemon rind and juice to sliced fragrant Angelys or Comice pears for extra flavour and balance in the pudding. This can be prepared ahead of time, but for best results, cook it so it comes fresh from the oven to the table. Just before you sit down to dinner, pour the vanilla-scented custard over the prepared croissant and pear mixture and pop it in the oven to bake while you eat and relax.

Pear & almond croissant pudding

SERVES 6
WINE SUGGESTION: MOSCATO D'ASTI
BEST IN AUTUMN/WINTER

300ml cream

250ml milk

1 vanilla bean

2 tbsp sugar

3 almond croissants, sliced into 4–5 pieces

3 ripe Angelys pears, peeled, cored and sliced

4 eggs, beaten

1 lemon, juice and grated zest

Preheat the oven to 180°C.

Combine the cream and milk in a saucepan, add the vanilla bean and sugar. Bring to simmering point then turn off the heat and leave to stand for 30 minutes to infuse the vanilla flavour.

Meanwhile, place the sliced croissants in a well-buttered, attractive ovenproof baking dish, overlapping the slices. Sprinkle the pears with the lemon juice and zest, and then add them to the croissants, tucking them in between the croissant slices.

Add the strained, infused milk and cream to the eggs. Beat well, then pour over the croissants and pears. Bake for 30–40 minutes until the custard is set and the pudding is puffy and golden.

Serve immediately with yogurt or whipped cream.

Based on a medieval recipe, the original 'posset' was never a dessert but just a warm nourishing drink, made with milk that was heated and then curdled with wine. This more recent version has become a favourite English dessert, incredibly easy to make and loved by every age group. The lemon makes it really tangy and it is as light as a feather to eat.

Lemon posset with mandarin

SERVES 4
WINE SUGGESTION: LATE-HARVEST RIESLING OR A SMALL SHOT OF LIMONCELLO
BEST IN AUTUMN/WINTER

500ml cream

150g caster sugar

75ml lemon juice

2 tsp grated lemon rind

2 mandarins

Put the cream into a saucepan and add the sugar. Stir with a wooden spoon to dissolve the sugar as the cream comes to the boil. Reduce the heat so the cream is at a very gentle simmer for 3 minutes. Make sure it does not rise up and bubble over.

Remove from the heat and stir in the lemon juice and the rind. When slightly cooled pour into tiny ramekins or little glasses and leave in the refrigerator overnight or for at least two hours to set.

To serve, peel the mandarins and remove as much pith as possible. Cut slices through the middle of each mandarin with a sharp knife and place a slice on each pot or glass of lemon posset.

Growing up I was never a fan of rice pudding but became entranced when we baked it in a cooking-school lesson. The creamy texture the baked rice took on as it slowly absorbed the milk was a revelation. This version uses coconut and rosewater to give the pudding much more flavour than the original. If you can't get strawberries you could always use canned stone fruit, in any season.

Coconut & rosewater rice puddings with strawberries

SERVES 4–6
WINE SUGGESTION: LATE-HARVEST RIESLING
BEST IN SPRING/SUMMER

80g short-grain rice
500ml Half and Half (or a mixture of milk and cream)
500ml coconut milk
4 tbsp sugar
1 tbsp rosewater
2 punnets strawberries

Put the rice in a sieve and rinse under running cold water. Shake dry and then place in a heavy-bottomed saucepan with the Half and Half (or milk and cream) and coconut milk. Bring to the boil while stirring, then reduce the heat so the rice is very gently simmering. Simmer for about 35–40 minutes, stirring often so the rice doesn't catch on the bottom.

When the rice is soft and the liquid is almost all absorbed, stir in 2 tablespoons of the sugar and the rosewater and allow to cool.

Meanwhile remove the tops from one punnet of the strawberries and purée them in a blender with the remaining sugar.

To serve, stir a little of the purée to streak through the rice pudding and spoon it into small glasses. Spoon more of the purée on top of the pudding. Slice the second punnet of strawberries and place a portion of strawberries on top to completely fill the glass. Chill until needed.

One of my favourite childhood desserts, Spanish cream, is at its best when it separates out so that there is a layer of milky jelly on the bottom, topped by a more frothy, bubbly custard-like cream. I have really fond memories of my mother making this proudly when her own mother came to dinner. I guess you could call it a family heirloom recipe. It is a lovely, light, prepare-ahead dessert and here I have added an extra layer of jelly and berries in the bottom of the dish to make it festive.

Spanish cream with berries

SERVES 8–10
WINE SUGGESTION: CHAMPAGNE
BEST IN SUMMER

2 punnets blueberries

2 punnets raspberries

1 packet blueberry or blackberry jelly crystals

500ml boiling water

3 cups full cream milk

20g gelatine

4 tbsp water

1 vanilla pod

3 eggs, separated

120g caster sugar

pinch of salt

200ml cream

Combine one punnet of raspberries with one punnet of the blueberries into a glass bowl.

Dissolve the jelly crystals in the boiling water, allow it to cool a little before pouring over the berries. Place in the refrigerator and leave until set.

To make the Spanish cream, pour the milk into a saucepan, split the vanilla pod and add to the milk, then heat until it almost reaches boiling point.

Soak the gelatine in 4 tablespoons of water in a small pan.

Meanwhile separate the eggs into two bowls. Beat the egg yolks with the sugar until thick and creamy using a whisk, adding a small pinch of salt. Add the hot milk to the yolk mixture and return this to the rinsed-out saucepan.

Place the gelatine over a low heat, watching carefully, heating it until is just melting. Do not let this boil as this will make the pudding lumpy. Add the dissolved gelatine to the mixture, stirring continuously with a wooden spoon over the low heat until the mixture thickens and coats the back of a spoon. Do not let this boil or even bubble, as the mixture will curdle.

Whisk the egg whites until stiff in a separate bowl, then fold them into the milk mixture while it is still warm. When almost cool but still not setting, pour it on top of the jelly. Place in the refrigerator overnight to set. The custard will separate out from the milky jelly, leaving several layers in your bowl.

To serve, softly whip the cream and spread over the Spanish cream. Decorate the top with the remaining berries.

One of the delights of growing up in a family is the memory of baking. I loved being in their kitchens when my mother or my grandmother baked cakes and cookies. My paternal grandmother, Nana Nancy, was a First World War bride, lured to a life in New Zealand by her Kiwi soldier husband. They'd met in the Warrington post office in Lancashire. I loved that she brought with her the great British baking traditions and this cookie recipe is from her kitchen to mine, via my own mother who often baked it, too.

Frosted brown sugar cookies

MAKES ABOUT 25 COOKIES
BEST IN ALL SEASONS

120g butter

200g brown sugar

2 egg yolks

200g wholemeal flour

1 tsp baking powder

pinch of salt

1 tsp pure vanilla essence

For the topping:

2 egg whites

150g brown sugar

½ tsp pure vanilla essence

Preheat the oven to 150°C.

Prepare a Swiss-roll tin by greasing with butter. Beat the butter and brown sugar together with an electric mixer until light and fluffy. Add the egg yolks while continuing to beat. Fold in the flour with the baking powder and the vanilla essence. Spread this mixture into the tin to form the base.

Clean the bowl and the beaters and beat the egg whites until they foam up and thicken. Add the brown sugar and vanilla essence. Continue beating until the mixture is light and fluffy. Spread this evenly over the base.

Bake in the heated oven for 30 minutes until the top is set. The middle will be chewy and moist. Cool before slicing into squares.

When fig season comes around it's always a race to get to the tree before the birds devour every ripe fig that appears. Luckily, unlike other fruit, figs on each branch ripen one by one, so if you do have a fig tree, you have a continuous supply for several weeks in the autumn. I love this recipe. I save the biggest figs in the fridge until I have enough to make a clafoutis. Choose a floral-flavoured honey to enhance the figgy flavour more intensely.

Fig & honey clafoutis

SERVES 4–6
WINE MATCH: LATE-HARVEST RIESLING
BEST IN AUTUMN

10–12 fresh ripe figs

3 large eggs

4 tbsp flour

3 tbsp honey

300ml whole milk

100ml cream

Preheat the oven to 160°C.

Generously butter a shallow ovenproof baking dish approximately 22cm diameter.

Wash and dry the figs and cut each in half lengthwise. Place cut-side up in the dish.

Beat the eggs, honey and flour in a bowl until smooth but not too bubbly. Stir in the milk and cream and combine well, keeping the consistency smooth.

Pour this batter around the figs so that it almost covers but not swamps them.

Place the dish in the oven and cook for about 45 minutes until the custard is set and the clafoutis puffs up a little and turns golden brown.

Remove from the oven, allow it to cool a little and serve with whipped cream or plain unsweetened yogurt.

THANKS

The past seven years have been a delightful food adventure – hard work but really enjoyable – to get those food columns finished and delivered weekly to the *Listener* team. My sincere thanks goes to chief editor Pamela Stirling, who has had faith in me, allowed me to work unimpeded and continues to be a joy to work with. The team at the *Listener* do a great job: subeditors, designers, and the art director, Derek Ward. They are always sympathetic and quick to respond to any last-minute changes. When I started at the *Listener* it was published by APN in the old *New Zealand Herald* offices, and there was seamless change as they continued to uphold the same high standards of journalism and production when it became part of the Bauer group. It is an honour to have this place to share New Zealand food stories.

I have a small, regular team I love working with and am very grateful to know. Liz Clarkson shot all the photos in this book and I am lucky to work with such a talented photographer. She is always calm, has a great eye and takes beautiful shots.

The vibrant and vivacious Kate Arbuthnot is the most stylish woman I know – the perfect person to style our shots. Kate always manages to turn up with the most appropriate and beautiful things to enhance the food, often travelling the tedious route from her home in Matakana to reach the shoot on time.

We are very grateful to the businesses who loan their fine tableware for use as props to enhance our photos. Thanks especially to Quail Farm Collectables, Green With Envy, Mooi Mooi, Morgan Haines, Vicky Fanning of Frolic Ceramics, The Red Barn, Old School Inc., and Matakana Home, all in the Matakana region, and Indie Home Collective, The Homestore and Millie's, in Auckland.

Also thanks to Gay Dobbie who willingly shows up when she's needed to wash up and assist on our shoots. And to Kathy Paterson, a brilliant food writer, cook, friend and confidante, whose work I really admire.

I have numerous friends to be thankful for in the food world. I have been a member, including a term as president, of the New Zealand Guild of Food Writers for nearly 30 years, and have enjoyed and benefitted from conferences, workshops and conversations where there has been much to share and learn about both our food and the professional side of being a food writer.

I was also on the inaugural executive of EatNZ, an association that aims to raise the profile of our amazing food scene in New Zealand. I love the possibilities that that might bring for local and international recognition. I am grateful to have played a part in getting that group established.

I have a small group of artisan producers and growers with whom I regularly get together to eat and talk food, and I love these crazy lunches and dinners. Their banter helps to firm up ideas and provide inspiration. Thanks for your friendship.

I am also privileged through my membership and past-president status of an international food professional association, IACP, which is connected to many of the world's great food writers and cookbook authors. Over the past 20 years there has been a ton of stuff to learn and become involved with on trips and at conferences, and some great, lasting culinary friendships made.

My mother has been a constant source of inspiration and support. It is wonderful to see her at 95 years of age continuing to look after herself, cooking daily and offering wise criticism when food is not 'tasty' enough. I love you, Mother.

And I cannot leave out my own loving family. My husband Murray willingly joins me on exploratory research food trips and meals. He happily eats the results of my recipe testing, even when he'd far rather have fish and salad. Our children, Katie, and Scott and his wife Loretta, have always been honest critics and most appreciative of my cooking. It's great to see them entertaining and presenting tasty fare to friends and family.

This book came about during a bus trip in Marlborough. Robbie Burton of Potton & Burton happened to be sitting beside me as we drove to a Cloudy Bay luncheon, and he expressed interest in the concept of this book. I am grateful to him and very appreciative of the team at one of New Zealand's best publishing houses who have worked on this project.

Most of all, I am grateful to my readers. I love being contacted by email with feedback on my columns, or bailed up in the aisles of the supermarket by enthusiastic cooks who are cooking and enjoying the latest recipes. Print media is the best, far better than the immediacy of social media where everyone is a self-appointed critic, whether they're qualified or not.

Long may magazines and books continue to be relevant and read by us all.

INSPIRATION, FOOD HEROES & SUPPLIERS

Often asked where I get my inspiration from for my weekly columns, I'd say seasonal food is my first and most important focus. But many of my ideas also come from places I visit and travel to, the restaurants and cafés I eat in, books and magazines I read, and just talking food with other food lovers.

My food heroes are many. I admire a lot of chefs, both in New Zealand and other countries, who cook terrific food and create interesting dishes that indicate the leading edge of innovation. I have a library of over 1000 cookbooks and find there's a handful of them that I go to constantly. Stephanie Alexander's *The Cooks Companion, The Constance Spry Cookbook, Vegetables from Amaranth to Zucchini* by Elizabeth Schneider and titles by Madhur Jaffrey, Alice Waters, Julia Child, Jane Grigson, Diana Henry and Deborah Madison are among ones I refer to most often.

As I have written elsewhere in this book, shopping for food is a large part of the cooking process. I spend my time divided between two places: the house we bought 42 years ago in central Auckland and a bach built 15 years ago in the popular Matakana region. Both places are well situated for buying fresh, delicious produce and ingredients.

When we first started going to Omaha Beach there was just a dairy, a butcher and a bakery. Now there's a thriving Saturday farmers' market, a beautifully constructed village with any number of specialist shops, cafés, restaurants and food purveyors, and a well-stocked grocery/deli store. But even better, the road from Matakana to Omaha Beach passes through the Omaha Flats, an area known as one of the most fertile growing regions in the whole country. Along that road at the height of summer there may be up to a dozen farm stands with honesty boxes where I can buy gorgeous farm-grown fruit and vegetables to cook with and for inspiration.

When at home in Auckland I live quite close to the Remuera shops, and while there's not the range of small shopkeepers that supplied me 42 years ago when we arrived, there's what I have called a 'golden triangle of shopping'. The local New World supermarket in Clonbern Rd is one of the best around, stocked extensively with organics, and the owner Adrian Barkla is open to any suggestions I have for adding fine products to his shelves. Across the road, Jack and Carrie Lum have operated a fine fruit-and-vegetable store, Jack Lum & Co, for the entire time I have lived in the district, and next door to them, the 4 & 20 Bakery produces the best sourdough bread and other treats. If I need specialty fresh fish I can get it from a superb fish shop, Remuera Fisheries. Without all these guys I would not be so inspired.

I am also inspired by the array of food producers who have poured their hearts and souls into some very fine food. We have a world-class farming industry in New Zealand as we grow grass year-round and have excellent rainfall in most regions. Our dairy and meat industries have held the economy together for 150 years and we're now seeing some excellent boutique producers throughout the country making fine products with worthy back-stories. I support boutique foods where I can.

I have listed here many of my favourite producers, those whose products I have used in these recipes and which I constantly buy. They are well worth seeking out and requesting in your own local supermarket. Most can be ordered online too.

Bostocks
bostocksorganic.co.nz
Organic free-range chicken

Clevedon Buffalo Cheese Company
clevedonbuffalo.co.nz
Making superb mozzarella, fresh cheese and ricotta

Cloudy Bay Clams
cloudybayclams.com
Fresh, sustainably harvested fresh clams in shell

Coastal Spring Lamb
coastalspringlamb.co.nz
Spring lamb from coastal family farms around New Zealand

Culley's
culleys.co.nz
Spicy range of hot sauces

Curious Croppers Tomatoes
curiouscroppers.co.nz
Growers of heritage tomatoes

Genevieve's Dressings
genevieves.co.nz
Fresh vinaigrettes, dressings, parfaits and mousses

Kapiti Cheese & Icecreams
tastekapiti.co.nz
Fonterra's range of premium cheeses

Lewis Road Creamery
lewisroadcreamery.co.nz
Innovative range of milk, cream and beverages, and cultured butter

Lot 8 Olive Oils
lot8.co.nz
A range of extra virgin and excellent cold-pressed flavoured oils

Ludbrook House
ludbrook.co.nz
Hand-made range of preserved lemons and figs, jams, etc

Mahurangi Oysters
mahurangioysters.co.nz
Fresh oysters in the shell grown in the Mahurangi Harbour

NZ King Salmon
kingsalmon.co.nz
Fresh and Manuka-smoked salmon sold under Regal and Ora King brands

Paneton
panetonbakery.co.nz
French bakery making many frozen specialties, including pre-rolled puff pastry

Pinoli
pinoli.co.nz
Marlborough-grown, fresh pine nuts

Sabato
sabato.co.nz
Importers of excellent Spanish and Italian products and fine cheeses and stockists of boutique NZ produce

Te Mana Lamb
temanalamb.com
Superb range of lamb cuts from the mountainous Southern Alps region

Uncle Joe's
unclejoes.co.nz
Fresh walnuts, hazelnuts, nut oils

Zany Zeus
zanyzeus.co.nz
Great range of fresh dairy products including haloumi, feta, ricotta, crème fraîche and more

INDEX

A

almonds
almond croissants: Pear & almond croissant pudding 212
Fig, blue cheese & bacon salad 74
Fresh apricot & ricotta tart 190
Griestorte with fresh strawberries 208

anchovies: Leg of lamb with minty feta sauce 128

apples
Braised red cabbage with spicy pork chops 146
Caramelised rhubarb & apple tart with compote 206
Chicken livers with shallots & apples 162
Kohlrabi & apple salad 38
Pork shoulder with apple & parsley stuffing 142

apricots
Fresh apricot & ricotta tart 190
Tray-baked chicken with potatoes & apricots 180

asparagus
Hāpuku, shiitake & asparagus stir-fry 94
Salmon in a spring vegetable broth 90
Spring green salad 12
Spring risotto with asparagus & broad beans 54

aubergines
Aubergine & pepper stew with chickpeas & basil 26
Baked aubergine, tomato & mozzarella 60
Roasted aubergine with red onions, yogurt & lemon 28

avocados
Avocado & caramelised pineapple salad 14
Avocado & gin-and-lime cured salmon 98
Kahawai ceviche with radishes, beetroot & avocado 102
Sardine & egg salad 20
Venison sliders 154

B

bacon
Bacon & egg fried rice 65
Cabbage & pork rolls in savoury broth 144
Cabbage, bacon & potato soup 76
Chicken, leek & bacon pie 170
Fig, blue cheese & bacon salad 74
Pork shoulder with apple & parsley stuffing 142

Baked aubergine, tomato & mozzarella 60

Baked chicken, leek & pumpkin 182

Baked kale with potatoes, olives & garlic 34

basil
Aubergine & pepper stew with chickpeas & basil 26
Baked aubergine, tomato & mozzarella 60
Courgettes with spaghetti, basil & cheese 70
Lamb salad with radish, watercress & watermelon 124

beans
see also broad beans; butter beans
Herbed lamb in a vegetable ragout 126
Three-bean salad with lemon & sliced duck breast 184

beef
Beef meatballs in spicy tomato sauce 136
Roast sirloin of beef with horseradish gravy 135
Star anise marinated beef 138

beetroot
Grilled vegetable & black rice salad 24
Kahawai ceviche with radishes, beetroot & avocado 102
Rice & quinoa salad with beetroot & carrots 40
Venison salad with pine nuts, feta & beetroot 152
Venison sliders 154

biscuits
Cheese straws 78
Crisp cheesy biscuits 78
Frosted brown sugar cookies 220

black rice: Grilled vegetable & black rice salad 24

blue cheese
Avocado & caramelised pineapple salad 14
Blue cheese & caramelised onion quiche 80
Fig, blue cheese & bacon salad 74
Persimmon & salami salad with balsamic dressing 36

blueberries
Blueberry syllabub 192
Raspberry & chocolate meringue tangle 204
Spanish cream with berries 218

Braised red cabbage with spicy pork chops 146

bread pudding: Cheesy cauliflower & leek bread pudding 82

broad beans
Chicken dumplings with braised broad beans, lemon & mint 168
Herbed lamb in a vegetable ragout 126
Roasted fennel & prawn salad 18
Salmon in a spring vegetable broth 90
Spring green salad 12
Spring risotto with asparagus & broad beans 54
Three-bean salad with lemon & sliced duck breast 184

broccoli sprouts: Japanese spring soba noodles 62

butter beans: Three-bean salad with lemon & sliced duck breast 184

Buttery braised fennel 46

cabbage
Braised red cabbage with spicy pork chops 146
Cabbage & pork rolls in savoury broth 144
Cabbage, bacon & potato soup 76

cakes
Chocolate cupcakes with salted caramel sauce 200
Griestorte with fresh strawberries 208

capsicums *see peppers*

caramel
Caramel notes 199
Chocolate cupcakes with salted caramel sauce 200

Caramelised rhubarb & apple tart with compote 206

carrots
Carrot, cheese & coriander fritters 30
Chicken & vegetable soup 166
Duck & mandarin ragout 186
Grilled vegetable & black rice salad 24
Herbed lamb in a vegetable ragout 126
Japanese spring soba noodles 62
Rice & quinoa salad with beetroot & carrots 40
Roasted fennel & prawn salad 18
Venison sliders 154

Casseroled chicken with fennel, potatoes, olives & preserved lemon 172

cauliflower
Cheesy cauliflower & leek bread pudding 82
Roasted golden cauliflower 50
Warm cauliflower salad 48

cavolo nero
Baked kale with potatoes, olives & garlic 34

Sausage, cavolo nero & fresh tomato pasta 84

celery
Chicken & vegetable soup 166
Duck & mandarin ragout 186

ceviche
Gurnard ceviche with melon & seaweed 100
Kahawai ceviche with radishes, beetroot & avocado 102

cheese
see also blue cheese; cream cheese; feta cheese; goat cheese; Grana Padano cheese; mozzarella cheese; parmesan cheese; pecorino; ricotta
Buttery braised fennel 46
Cheese straws 78
Cheesy cauliflower & leek bread pudding 82
Crisp cheesy biscuits 78
Spring risotto with asparagus & broad beans 54

chicken
Baked chicken, leek & pumpkin 182
Casseroled chicken with fennel, potatoes, olives & preserved lemon 172
Chicken & vegetable soup 166
Chicken dumplings with braised broad beans, lemon & mint 168
Chicken, leek & bacon pie 170
Miso caramel chicken nibbles 160
Poussins with pears & parsley 178
Roast chicken salad with nectarines & summer leaves 164
Tray-baked chicken with potatoes & apricots 180
The ultimate roast chicken 176

Chicken livers with shallots & apples 162

chickpeas: Aubergine & pepper stew with chickpeas & basil 26

Chilli sauce 116

chives: Oyster & chive frittata 112

chocolate
Chocolate cupcakes with salted caramel sauce 200
Chocolate meringues with chocolate cream 210
Raspberry & chocolate meringue tangle 204

chowder: Mussel & salmon chowder 120

clafoutis: Fig & honey clafoutis 222

clams
Clams with corn & chilli 116
Portuguese-style clam stew 104

Classic custard 198

Classic French vinaigrette 17

coconut cream & milk
Coconut & rosewater rice puddings with strawberries 216
Coconut custard 198
Salmon & cucumber green curry 118

cookies: Frosted brown sugar cookies 220

coriander
Carrot, cheese & coriander fritters 30
Flavours of Asia dressing 17
Portuguese-style clam stew 104
Rajasthan lamb curry 130
Roast venison with spinach, dates & orange 156
Salmon & cucumber green curry 118

corn
Clams with corn & chilli 116
Grilled vegetable & black rice salad 24

courgettes
Courgettes with spaghetti, basil & cheese 70
Grilled vegetable & black rice salad 24

cream cheese: Caramelised rhubarb & apple tart with compote 206

Creamy oyster & leek soup 106

crème fraîche: Strawberry & crème fraîche tartlets 194

Crisp cheesy biscuits 78

229

crumbed food: Perfect crumbed food 65

cucumber
    Miso caramel chicken nibbles 160
    Rice & quinoa salad with beetroot & carrots 40
    Salmon & cucumber green curry 118

cupcakes: Chocolate cupcakes with salted caramel sauce 200

curries
    Rajasthan lamb curry 130
    Salmon & cucumber green curry 118

custard
    Classic custard 198
    Coconut custard 198

D

dates: Roast venison with spinach, dates & orange 156

dressings
    Classic French vinaigrette 17
    Flavours of Asia dressing 17
    Herb dressing 116
    Miso dressing 62
    Orange & honey vinaigrette 17

duck
    Duck & mandarin ragout 186
    Three-bean salad with lemon & sliced duck breast 184

E

eggplants *see aubergines*

eggs
    Bacon & egg fried rice 65
    Blue cheese & caramelised onion quiche 80
    Cheesy cauliflower & leek bread pudding 82
    Classic custard 198
    Coconut custard 198
    Lemon delicious 202
    Oyster & chive frittata 112
    Pear & almond croissant pudding 212

Roast leek, mandarin & egg salad 42
Salmon coulibiac 114
Sardine & egg salad 20
Spanish cream with berries 218
Spinach tart 72
Whitebait fritters 88

F

fennel
    Avocado & gin-and-lime cured salmon 98
    Buttery braised fennel 46
    Casseroled chicken with fennel, potatoes, olives & preserved lemon 172
    Chicken & vegetable soup 166
    Mussel & salmon chowder 120
    Orange, fennel & pomegranate salad 44
    Roasted fennel & prawn salad 18
    Salmon & cucumber green curry 118
    Tray-baked chicken with potatoes & apricots 180

feta cheese
    Carrot, cheese & coriander fritters 30
    Cheesy cauliflower & leek bread pudding 82
    Leg of lamb with minty feta sauce 128
    Pea, parsley, mint & feta fritters 68
    Venison salad with pine nuts, feta & beetroot 152
    Warm cauliflower salad 48

Fig & honey clafoutis 222
Fig, blue cheese & bacon salad 74

fish
    see also prawns; salmon; shellfish
    Gurnard ceviche with melon & seaweed 100
    Hāpuku, shiitake & asparagus stir-fry 94
    Kahawai ceviche with radishes, beetroot & avocado 102
    Kingfish carpaccio 92
    tips for pan-frying 97
    Turmeric & lime fish fillets 110

Flavours of Asia dressing 17
French vinaigrette 17
Fresh apricot & ricotta tart 190
Fresh salmon with yuzu oil & garden herbs 108
Fried tofu with spicy minced pork 140
frittata: Oyster & chive frittata 112

fritters
    Carrot, cheese & coriander fritters 30
    Pea, parsley, mint & feta fritters 68
    Whitebait fritters 88

Frosted brown sugar cookies 220
Fruit salad 197

G

garlic
    Aubergine & pepper stew with chickpeas & basil 26
    Baked kale with potatoes, olives & garlic 34
    Tray-baked chicken with potatoes & apricots 180

ginger, crystallised: Rhubarb compote with pomegranate syrup & ginger 206

goat cheese
    Tomato & goat cheese tart 58
    Venison salad with pine nuts, feta & beetroot 152

Grana Padano cheese
    Duck & mandarin ragout 186
    Spring risotto with asparagus & broad beans 54

gravy
    How to make a good gravy 134
    Roast sirloin of beef with horseradish gravy 135

Griestorte with fresh strawberries 208
Grilled vegetable & black rice salad 24
Gurnard ceviche with melon & seaweed 100

H

Ham, mozzarella & tomato salad 22

ham: Spring risotto with asparagus & broad beans 54

Hāpuku, shiitake & asparagus stir-fry 94

hazelnuts: Warm cauliflower salad 48

Herbed lamb in a vegetable ragout 126

Herbed Yorkshire puddings 135

herbs
see also individual herbs, e.g. parsley
Fresh salmon with yuzu oil & garden herbs 108
Herb dressing 116
Leg of lamb with minty feta sauce 128
Rice & quinoa salad with beetroot & carrots 40
Salmon coulibiac 114
The ultimate roast chicken 176

honey
Fig & honey clafoutis 222
Orange & honey vinaigrette 17

horopito pepper: Kumara gratin with horopito pepper 66

horseradish mustard: Roast sirloin of beef with horseradish gravy 135

hummus: Roasted golden cauliflower 50

J

Japanese spring soba noodles 62

K

Kahawai ceviche with radishes, beetroot & avocado 102

kale: Baked kale with potatoes, olives & garlic 34

Kingfish carpaccio 92

Kohlrabi & apple salad 38

kumara
Kumara gratin with horopito pepper 66
Pork shoulder with apple & parsley stuffing 142

L

lamb
Herbed lamb in a vegetable ragout 126
Lamb salad with radish, watercress & watermelon 124
Lamb shanks with orange, tomato & olives 132
Leg of lamb with minty feta sauce 128
Rajasthan lamb curry 130

leeks
Baked chicken, leek & pumpkin 182
Cheesy cauliflower & leek bread pudding 82
Chicken, leek & bacon pie 170
Creamy oyster & leek soup 106
Roast leek, mandarin & egg salad 42

lemons
see also preserved lemons
Chicken dumplings with braised broad beans, lemon & mint 168
Chicken, leek & bacon pie 170
Griestorte with fresh strawberries 208
Kahawai ceviche with radishes, beetroot & avocado 102
Lamb salad with radish, watercress & watermelon 124
Lemon delicious 202
Lemon posset with mandarin 214
Roasted aubergine with red onions, yogurt & lemon 28
Three-bean salad with lemon & sliced duck breast 184

lettuce
Ham, mozzarella & tomato salad 22
Persimmon & salami salad with balsamic dressing 36
Roast chicken salad with nectarines & summer leaves 164
Sardine & egg salad 20
Spring green salad 12
Venison sliders 154
Venison winter salad 150

limes
Avocado & gin-and-lime cured salmon 98
Carrot, cheese & coriander fritters 30
Chicken livers with shallots & apples 162
Flavours of Asia dressing 17
Gurnard ceviche with melon & seaweed 100
Salmon & cucumber green curry 118
Turmeric & lime fish fillets 110

M

mandarins
Duck & mandarin ragout 186
Lemon posset with mandarin 214
Roast leek, mandarin & egg salad 42

mascarpone: Blue cheese & caramelised onion quiche 80

meatballs: Beef meatballs in spicy tomato sauce 136

melon
Gurnard ceviche with melon & seaweed 100
Lamb salad with radish, watercress & watermelon 124

meringues
Chocolate meringues with chocolate cream 210
Raspberry & chocolate meringue tangle 204

mesclun *see salad leaves*

microgreens: Miso caramel chicken nibbles 160

mint
Chicken dumplings with braised broad beans, lemon & mint 168
Ham, mozzarella & tomato salad 22

Herbed lamb in a vegetable ragout 126
Leg of lamb with minty feta sauce 128
Orange & honey vinaigrette 17
Orange, fennel & pomegranate salad 44
Pea, parsley, mint & feta fritters 68
Roast leek, mandarin & egg salad 42
Roast venison with spinach, dates & orange 156
Roasted golden cauliflower 50
Tray-baked chicken with potatoes & apricots 180
The ultimate roast chicken 176
Venison salad with pine nuts, feta & beetroot 152
Warm cauliflower salad 48

Miso caramel chicken nibbles 160
Miso dressing 62

mozzarella cheese
Baked aubergine, tomato & mozzarella 60
Ham, mozzarella & tomato salad 22

mushrooms
Cabbage & pork rolls in savoury broth 144
Chicken, leek & bacon pie 170
Hāpuku, shiitake & asparagus stir-fry 94
Japanese spring soba noodles 62
Mushroom risotto 56

Mussel & salmon chowder 120

N

nectarines: Roast chicken salad with nectarines & summer leaves 164

noodles
Chicken & vegetable soup 166
Duck and mandarin ragout 186
Japanese spring soba noodles 62

O

olives
Baked chicken, leek & pumpkin 182
Baked kale with potatoes, olives & garlic 34
Casseroled chicken with fennel, potatoes, olives & preserved lemon 172
Lamb shanks with orange, tomato & olives 132
Roast leek, mandarin & egg salad 42

onions
Aubergine & pepper stew with chickpeas & basil 26
Blue cheese & caramelised onion quiche 80
Braised red cabbage with spicy pork chops 146
Portuguese-style clam stew 104
Roast chicken salad with nectarines & summer leaves 164
Roasted aubergine with red onions, yogurt & lemon 28

oranges
Lamb shanks with orange, tomato & olives 132
Orange & honey vinaigrette 17
Orange, fennel & pomegranate salad 44
Pork shoulder with apple & parsley stuffing 142
Roast venison with spinach, dates & orange 156
Spring green salad 12

oysters
Creamy oyster & leek soup 106
Oyster & chive frittata 112

P

parmesan cheese
Cheese straws 78
Courgettes with spaghetti, basil & cheese 70
Crisp cheesy biscuits 78
Kumara gratin with horopito pepper 66
Oyster & chive frittata 112
Spinach tart 72

parsley
Bacon & egg fried rice 65
Beef meatballs in spicy tomato sauce 136
Chicken & vegetable soup 166
Chicken livers with shallots & apples 162
Duck & mandarin ragout 186
Fig, blue cheese & bacon salad 74
Herb dressing 116
Herbed lamb in a vegetable ragout 126
Herbed Yorkshire puddings 135
Kohlrabi & apple salad 38
Lamb shanks with orange, tomato & olives 132
Mushroom risotto 56
Pea, parsley, mint & feta fritters 68
Pork shoulder with apple & parsley stuffing 142
Poussins with pears & parsley 178
Roasted fennel & prawn salad 18
Sardine & egg salad 20
The ultimate roast chicken 176
Venison salad with pine nuts, feta & beetroot 152
Venison sliders 154
Venison winter salad 150

pasta
Courgettes with spaghetti, basil & cheese 70
Duck & mandarin ragout 186
Lamb shanks with orange, tomato & olives 132
Sausage, cavolo nero & fresh tomato pasta 84

pears
Pear & almond croissant pudding 212
Poussins with pears & parsley 178

peas
Chicken & vegetable soup 166
Ham, mozzarella & tomato salad 22
Pea, parsley, mint & feta fritters 68
Salmon in a spring vegetable broth 90
Spring risotto with asparagus & broad beans 54

pecorino: Sausage, cavolo nero & fresh tomato pasta 84

peppers
    Aubergine & pepper stew with chickpeas & basil 26
    Beef meatballs in spicy tomato sauce 136
    Chilli sauce 116
    Grilled vegetable & black rice salad 24
    Rice & quinoa salad with beetroot & carrots 40

Perfect crumbed food 65

persimmons
    Persimmon & salami salad with balsamic dressing 36
    Venison winter salad 150

pies
    Chicken, leek & bacon pie 170
    Salmon coulibiac 114

pine nuts
    Gurnard ceviche with melon & seaweed 100
    Rice & quinoa salad with beetroot & carrots 40
    Roast squash wedges with pine nuts, yogurt & sumac 32
    Venison salad with pine nuts, feta & beetroot 152

pineapple: Avocado & caramelised pineapple salad 14

pink peppercorns
    Gurnard ceviche with melon & seaweed 100
    Kingfish carpaccio 92

pomegranate arils
    Leg of lamb with minty feta sauce 128
    Orange, fennel & pomegranate salad 44

pomegranate syrup: Rhubarb compote with pomegranate syrup & ginger 206

pork
    Braised red cabbage with spicy pork chops 146
    Cabbage & pork rolls in savoury broth 144
    Fried tofu with spicy minced pork 140
    Pork braised in milk 148
    Pork shoulder with apple & parsley stuffing 142
    Sausage, cavolo nero & fresh tomato pasta 84

Portuguese-style clam stew 104

potatoes
    Baked kale with potatoes, olives & garlic 34
    Best-ever roast potatoes 134
    Cabbage, bacon & potato soup 76
    Casseroled chicken with fennel, potatoes, olives & preserved lemon 172
    Mussel & salmon chowder 120
    Salmon & cucumber green curry 118
    Salmon in a spring vegetable broth 90
    Tray-baked chicken with potatoes & apricots 180

Poussins with pears & parsley 178

prawns: Roasted fennel & prawn salad 18

preserved lemons
    Baked chicken, leek & pumpkin 182
    Casseroled chicken with fennel, potatoes, olives & preserved lemon 172
    Fig, blue cheese & bacon salad 74
    Leg of lamb with minty feta sauce 128
    Roasted aubergine with red onions, yogurt & lemon 28
    Sardine & egg salad 20
    The ultimate roast chicken 176
    Tray-baked chicken with potatoes & apricots 180
    Warm cauliflower salad 48

pumpkin
    Baked chicken, leek & pumpkin 182
    Roast squash wedges with pine nuts, yogurt & sumac 32
    Venison winter salad 150

Q

quiches *see tarts & quiches*

quinoa: Rice & quinoa salad with beetroot & carrots 40

R

radicchio: Venison winter salad 150

radishes
    Kahawai ceviche with radishes, beetroot & avocado 102
    Lamb salad with radish, watercress & watermelon 124
    Sardine & egg salad 20

Rajasthan lamb curry 130

raspberries
    Raspberry & chocolate meringue tangle 204
    Spanish cream with berries 218

rhubarb
    Caramelised rhubarb & apple tart with compote 206
    Rhubarb compote with pomegranate syrup & ginger 206

rice
    Bacon & egg fried rice 65
    Coconut & rosewater rice puddings with strawberries 216
    Grilled vegetable & black rice salad 24
    Mushroom risotto 56
    Rice & quinoa salad with beetroot & carrots 40
    Salmon coulibiac 114
    Spring risotto with asparagus & broad beans 54

ricotta
    Fresh apricot & ricotta tart 190
    Spinach tart 72

risotto
    Mushroom risotto 56
    Spring risotto with asparagus & broad beans 54

Roast chicken salad with nectarines & summer leaves 164

Roast leek, mandarin & egg salad 42

Roast sirloin of beef with horseradish gravy 135
Roast squash wedges with pine nuts, yogurt & sumac 32
Roast venison with spinach, dates & orange 156
Roasted aubergine with red onions, yogurt & lemon 28
Roasted fennel & prawn salad 18
Roasted golden cauliflower 50

rocket
    Fig, blue cheese & bacon salad 74
    Grilled vegetable & black rice salad 24
    Miso caramel chicken nibbles 160
    Persimmon & salami salad with balsamic dressing 36
    Roasted fennel & prawn salad 18

rosemary
    Baked chicken, leek & pumpkin 182
    Leg of lamb with minty feta sauce 128

rosewater: Coconut & rosewater rice puddings with strawberries 216

S

sage: Cabbage & pork rolls in savoury broth 144

salad leaves
    see also microgreens; and individual types of leaves, e.g. rocket
    Avocado & caramelised pineapple salad 14
    Roasted fennel & prawn salad 18

salami: Persimmon & salami salad with balsamic dressing 36

salmon
    Avocado & gin-and-lime cured salmon 98
    Fresh salmon with yuzu oil & garden herbs 108
    Mussel & salmon chowder 120
    Salmon & cucumber green curry 118
    Salmon coulibiac 114
    Salmon in a spring vegetable broth 90

Salted caramel sauce 200
Sardine & egg salad 20

sauces
    Chilli sauce 116
    Chocolate sauce 204
    Salted caramel sauce 200

sausages
    Portuguese-style clam stew 104
    Sausage, cavolo nero & fresh tomato pasta 84

seaweed: Gurnard ceviche with melon & seaweed 100

semolina: Griestorte with fresh strawberries 208

shallots
    Chicken livers with shallots & apples 162
    Spring risotto with asparagus & broad beans 54

shellfish
    Clams with corn & chilli 116
    Creamy oyster & leek soup 106
    Mussel & salmon chowder 120
    Oyster & chive frittata 112
    Portuguese-style clam stew 104

shiitake mushrooms
    Cabbage & pork rolls in savoury broth 144
    Hāpuku, shiitake & asparagus stir-fry 94

Simo's Orange & Cinnamon Zest: Lamb shanks with orange, tomato & olives 132

sliders: Venison sliders 154

snow peas
    Herbed lamb in a vegetable ragout 126
    Spring green salad 12

soba noodles: Japanese spring soba noodles 62

soup
    Cabbage, bacon & potato soup 76
    Chicken & vegetable soup 166
    Creamy oyster & leek soup 106
    Mussel & salmon chowder 120

spaghetti: Courgettes with spaghetti, basil & cheese 70

Spanish cream with berries 218

spinach
    Beef meatballs in spicy tomato sauce 136
    Roast venison with spinach, dates & orange 156
    Salmon & cucumber green curry 118
    Salmon coulibiac 114
    Spinach tart 72
    Venison salad with pine nuts, feta & beetroot 152
    Warm cauliflower salad 48

Spring green salad 12

Spring risotto with asparagus & broad beans 54

sprouts
    Fresh salmon with yuzu oil & garden herbs 108
    Japanese spring soba noodles 62
    Venison sliders 154

squash: Roast squash wedges with pine nuts, yogurt & sumac 32

Star anise marinated beef 138

strawberries
    Coconut & rosewater rice puddings with strawberries 216
    Griestorte with fresh strawberries 208
    Raspberry & chocolate meringue tangle 204
    Strawberry & crème fraîche tartlets 194

sugar snap peas: Salmon in a spring vegetable broth 90

sumac
    Roast squash wedges with pine nuts, yogurt & sumac 32
    Roasted aubergine with red onions, yogurt & lemon 28

syllabub: Blueberry syllabub 192

T

tarragon: Roast chicken salad with nectarines & summer leaves 164

tarts & quiches
Blue cheese & caramelised onion quiche 80
Spinach tart 72
Tomato & goat cheese tart 58

tarts, sweet
Caramelised rhubarb & apple tart with compote 206
Fresh apricot & ricotta tart 190
Strawberry & crème fraîche tartlets 194

Three-bean salad with lemon & sliced duck breast 184

thyme
Baked chicken, leek & pumpkin 182
Beef meatballs in spicy tomato sauce 136
Chicken dumplings with braised broad beans, lemon & mint 168
Chicken, leek & bacon pie 170
Herbed Yorkshire puddings 135
Lamb shanks with orange, tomato & olives 132
Roast sirloin of beef with horseradish gravy 135
Roast squash wedges with pine nuts, yogurt & sumac 32
Tomato & goat cheese tart 58

tofu: Fried tofu with spicy minced pork 140

tomatoes, canned
Beef meatballs in spicy tomato sauce 136
Fried tofu with spicy minced pork 140
Lamb shanks with orange, tomato & olives 132

tomatoes, fresh
Aubergine & pepper stew with chickpeas & basil 26
Baked aubergine, tomato & mozzarella 60
Cabbage & pork rolls in savoury broth 144
Chilli sauce 116

Ham, mozzarella & tomato salad 22
Portuguese-style clam stew 104
Sausage, cavolo nero & fresh tomato pasta 84
Tomato & goat cheese tart 58

Tray-baked chicken with potatoes & apricots 180

turmeric
Rice & quinoa salad with beetroot & carrots 40
Turmeric & lime fish fillets 110

V

venison
Roast venison with spinach, dates & orange 156
Venison salad with pine nuts, feta & beetroot 152
Venison sliders 154
Venison winter salad 150

vinaigrette
Classic French 17
Orange & honey vinaigrette 17

W

walnuts
Kohlrabi & apple salad 38
Venison winter salad 150
Caramelised rhubarb & apple tart with compote 206

Warm cauliflower salad 48

watercress
Avocado & gin-and-lime cured salmon 98
Lamb salad with radish, watercress & watermelon 124
Salmon in a spring vegetable broth 90
Spring green salad 12

watermelon: Lamb salad with radish, watercress & watermelon 124

Whitebait fritters 88

wine and food matching 174–75

Y

yogurt
Leg of lamb with minty feta sauce 128
Raspberry & chocolate meringue tangle 204
Roast squash wedges with pine nuts, yogurt & sumac 32
Roasted aubergine with red onions, yogurt & lemon 28
Roasted golden cauliflower 50

Yorkshire puddings 135

yuzu oil: Fresh salmon with yuzu oil & garden herbs 108

Z

zucchini *see courgettes*